THE REVELATIONS OF DIVINE LOVE
OF
JULIAN OF NORWICH

Translated by
JAMES WALSH, S.J.

ANTHONY CLARKE BOOKS
WHEATHAMPSTEAD — HERTFORDSHIRE

DE LICENTIA SUPERIORUM ORDINIS

NIHIL OBSTAT: CAROLUS DAVIS, S.T.L.
CENSOR DEPUTATUS
IMPRIMATUR: E. MORROGH BERNARD
VICARIUS GENERALIS
WESTMONASTERII: DIE 24a APRILIS 1961

The Nihil obstat *and* Imprimatur *are a declaration that a book or pamphlet is considered to be free from doctrinal or moral error. It is not implied that those who have granted the* Nihil obstat *and* Imprimatur *agree with the content, opinions or statements expressed.*

This translation © James Walsh, S.J., 1961

Reprinted 1973

This edition published 1980

ISBN: 0 85650 059 3

MADE AND PRINTED IN GREAT BRITAIN BY
THE GARDEN CITY PRESS LIMITED,
LETCHWORTH, HERTFORDSHIRE SG6 1JS
FOR ANTHONY CLARKE BOOKS
WHEATHAMSTEAD — HERTFORDSHIRE

THE REVELATIONS OF DIVINE LOVE
OF JULIAN OF NORWICH

PREFACE

IN spite of the fact that several printed editions of the *Revelations of Divine Love* have been offered to the public since Dom Serenus Cressy modernized the version of the Paris MS. in 1670, there has not yet appeared an edition which takes account of the twofold MS. tradition of the so-called Longer Version, exemplified in the three extant MSS.[1]: the sixteenth-century Paris MS. (Bibliothèque Nationale Fonds Anglais 40), and the British Museum Sloane MSS. (2499, mid-17th century, and 3705, late 17th century). Of the nineteenth-century editions, two are little more than reprints of Cressy, with the addition of Introductions by their respective editors, H. Collins (1877) and G. Tyrell (1902); the third, edited by G. H. Parker (1847), also derives through Cressy from the Paris MS. The more modern editions of Hudleston (Orchard Series 1927 and 1952) and Warrack (first published in 1902, and now in its 14th edition) are both versions of the Sloane MSS. Neither editor takes any account of the readings of the Paris MS.

Through the kindness of Sister Anna Maria Reynolds, C.P., M.A., Ph.D., who has made available to me her transcripts of all three MSS., this present edition represents a collation of Paris and Sloane. Sister Reynolds's conclusion (which I have accepted), that the Paris MSS. represents more nearly the MS. tradition, is borne out by the discovery of a late fifteenth-century *Florilegium* in the Westminster Cathedral Library, a compilation of extracts from Walter Hilton's commentaries on the Psalms *Qui Habitat* and *Bonum Est*, from his *Scale of Perfection* and from Julian's

---

[1] The fourth extant MS., the unique copy of the Shorter Version, stands outside this tradition. Cf. Introduction, p. 1, n. 1.

PREFACE

Revelations. The extracts from the *Revelations* consistently favour the readings of the Paris MS. against those of the Sloane MSS. I have therefore adopted Paris as the basis of my version, though I have never scrupled to substitute a reading from Sloane whenever this seemed superior, either linguistically or textually.

My choice of readings has been governed largely by what appear to me to be the principles of Julian's spiritual theology. In point of fact, I began my version in the settled conviction that there is nothing unorthodox, nothing contrary to Catholic theology, in the *Revelations*. As far as language is concerned, the mystics often find themselves balanced on a razor's edge between incomprehensibility and unorthodoxy; and Julian is no exception. Hence I have always tried to follow the advice of the scribe of the Sloane MS. 2499.

> This revelation is high divinity and high wisdom . . . beware that thou take not one thing and leave another, according to thine affection and thy liking, for that is the way of an heretic; but take everything with other . . .

My principle in translating has been to retain, wherever possible, the vocabulary and the syntax, as well as the idiom, the emphasis and especially the rhythm of the original, in the belief that Julian's Middle English is close enough to sixteenth-century English (on which we are all brought up, through Shakespeare, if not through the Authorized Version of the Bible) to be intelligible to the modern reader with the minimum of change. I believe also that the difficulty experienced in reading a text such as Julian's may be of advantage; unfamiliarity with idiom and construction forces the reader to weigh the author's words more carefully. Hence wherever I felt that the reader would understand the archaic word, expression or construction without too much difficulty, the original has been retained; but punctuation and spelling have been modernized throughout. Absolute consistency, even were it possible, has been considered undesirable, since some archaic forms act as an irritant to the modern reader. I have, however, taken the risk of consistently retaining the ending "—eth" in the third person singular of the present indicative, since to remove it would often involve the reconstruction of a phrase or the introduction of the expletive "do", with consequent loss of the essential rhythm. I have tried to avoid throughout what is perhaps the modernizer's greatest temptation—to improve his original.

The chapter headings are taken from the Sloane MSS. They do not occur in the Paris MS.

CONTENTS

CHAPTER	PAGE
Preface	v
Introduction	1
1. Of the number of the Revelations, in detail	45
2. Of the time of these Revelations; and how she asked three petitions	47
3. Of the sickness obtained of God by petition	49
4. Here beginneth the first Revelation, of the precious crowning of Christ, etc., as described in the first chapter; and how God filleth the heart full of the utmost joy; and of his great meekness; and how the sight of the passion of Christ is sufficient strength against every temptation of the fiends; and of the great excellence and meekness of the blessed Virgin Mary	51
5. How God is to us everything that is good, tenderly wrapping us round; and everything that is made is nothing in regard to Almighty God; and how man hath no rest until he counteth himself and all things as nothing, for the love of God	52
6. How we should pray; of the great tender love that our Lord hath to man's soul—wishing us to be occupied in the knowing and loving of him	54
7. How our Lady, beholding the greatness of her Maker, thought herself the least; and of the great drops of blood running from under the garland; and how man's greatest joy is that the most high and mighty God is the holiest and most courteous	57
8. A recapitulation of what is said; and how this was shewed to her for all in general	59
9. Of the meekness of this woman, keeping herself always in the faith of the Holy Church; and how	

CONTENTS

CHAPTER		PAGE
	he that loveth his even-christian for God, loveth all things	61
10.	The second Revelation is of his discolouring, etc.; of our redemption and the discolouring of the vernicle; and how it pleaseth God that we seek him earnestly, waiting on him steadfastly and trusting in him mightily	62
11.	The third Revelation, etc.; How God doeth all things except sin, never changing his purpose, without end; for he hath made all things in the fullness of his goodness	66
12.	The fourth Revelation, etc.; How it pleaseth God rather and better that we should wash us in his blood, from sin, than in water; for his blood is most precious	68
13.	The fifth Revelation sheweth that the temptation of the fiend is overcome by the passion of Christ; to the increase of joy in us, and to the fiend's pain, everlastingly	69
14.	The sixth Revelation is of the worshipful thanks with which he rewardeth his servants, and it hath three joys	71
15.	The seventh Revelation is of our oftentimes feeling weal and woe; and how it is expedient that a man sometimes be left without comfort, even when sin is not the cause	72
16.	The eighth Revelation is of the last piteous pains of Christ's dying, and the discolouring of his face, and the drying of his flesh	74
17.	Of the grievous bodily thirst of Christ, and its fourfold cause; of his piteous crowning, and of what giveth most pain to a true lover of his	75
18.	Of the Spiritual Martyrdom of our Lady and other lovers of Christ; and how all things, good and ill, suffered with him	77
19.	Of the comfortable beholding of the crucifix; and how the desire of the flesh without consent of the	

CONTENTS

CHAPTER		PAGE
	soul is no sin, and the flesh must be in pain, suffering until both be oned to Christ	79
20.	Of the ineffable passion of Christ, and of three things of the passion always to be remembered	80
21.	How we are now dying on the cross with Christ; but his looking on us putteth away all our pain	82
22.	The ninth Revelation is of the liking, etc.; of three heavens and the infinite love of Christ in his desiring every day to suffer for us, if he could; although it is not needful	83
23.	How Christ willeth that we rejoice with him greatly in our redemption, and that we desire grace from him that we may so do	85
24.	The tenth Revelation is our Lord Jesus shewing in love his blessed heart cloven in two, rejoicing	87
25.	The eleventh Revelation is a high ghostly shewing of his Mother	88
26.	The twelfth Revelation is that our Lord God is sovereign Being	90
27.	The thirteenth Revelation is that our Lord God willeth that we have great regard to all the deeds that he hath done—to the great nobleness that belongeth to the making of all things; and how sin is not known except by the pain	90
28.	How the children of salvation shall be shaken in sorrows, but Christ rejoiceth therein with compassion; of a remedy against tribulation	92
29.	Adam's sin was the greatest; but the satisfaction for it is more pleasing to God than ever the sin was harmful	94
30.	How we should have joy and trust in our Saviour, not presuming to know his secret counsels	94
31.	Of the longing and the spiritual thirst of Christ, which lasteth and shall last until doomsday; and by reason of his body, he is not yet fully glorified, nor all impassible	96
32.	How all things shall be well and Scripture fulfilled;	

CONTENTS

CHAPTER		PAGE
	and we must steadfastly hold us in the faith of Holy Church, as is Christ's will	98
33.	All damned souls are despised in the sight of God as the Devil is; and these Revelations do not take away the faith of Holy Church, but strengthen it; and the more we seek to know God's secrets, the less we know	100
34.	God sheweth the secrets necessary to his lovers; and how they please God much who receive diligently the preaching of Holy Church	101
35.	How God doeth all that is good, and worshipfully permitteth, by his mercy, all that shall cease to be when sin is no longer permitted	102
36.	Of another excellent deed that our Lord shall do, which by grace may be known, in part, here; and how we should have joy in the same; and how God still doeth miracles	104
37.	God keepeth his chosen full surely, although they sin; for in them is a godly will that never tasted sin	107
38.	The sin of the chosen shall be turned to joy and worship; example of David, Peter and John of Beverley	108
39.	Of the sharpness of sin and the goodness of contrition; and how our kind Lord willeth us not to despair	109
40.	It behoveth us to long in love with Jesus, eschewing sin for love; the vileness of sin surpasseth all pains; and God loveth us well and tenderly whilst we are in sin; and so must we behave towards our neighbour	111
41.	The fourteenth Revelation is as aforesaid; it is impossible that we should pray for mercy and lack it; and how God willeth us to pray always, though we be dry and barren, for that prayer is to him acceptable and pleasing	113
42.	Of three things that belong to prayer, and how we should pray; and of the goodness of God, that supplieth always for our imperfections and feebleness, when we do what we ought to do	116

CONTENTS

CHAPTER		PAGE
43.	What prayer doeth when ordained to God's will; and how the goodness of God hath great liking in the deeds that he doeth concerning us—as though he were beholden to us, working all things most sweetly	118
44.	Of the properties of the Trinity; and how man's soul, a creature, hath the same properties in doing that which it was made for—seeing, beholding and marvelling at its God; so that, to itself, it seemeth as naught	121
45.	Of the firm deep judgement of God, and the variable judgement of man	122
46.	We cannot know ourselves in this life except by faith and grace; but we must acknowledge ourselves sinners. And how God is never wroth, being most near the soul, it keeping	123
47.	We must reverently marvel, and meekly yield ourselves, ever enjoying in God; and how our blindness, in that we see not God, is the cause of sin	125
48.	Of mercy and grace; and their properties; and how we shall rejoice that ever we suffered woe patiently	127
49.	Our life is grounded in love; without the which we perish. God is never wroth, but in our wrath and sin, he mercifully keepeth us, and regarding our tribulations, treateth with us unto peace	129
50.	How the chosen soul was never dead in the sight of God: and of a marvel concerning the same. How three things emboldened her to ask of God the understanding of this	131
51.	The answer to the doubt aforesaid, by a marvellous parable of a lord and a servant; and God willeth that we abide his coming—for it was nearly twenty years after, ere she fully understood this parable. How it is to be understood that Christ sitteth on the right hand of the Father	132

CONTENTS

CHAPTER		PAGE
52.	God rejoiceth that he is our Father, Brother and Spouse. How the Chosen have here a mingling of weal and woe: but God is with us in three ways. And how we may eschew sin: but never perfectly, as in heaven	144
53.	The kindness of God assigneth no blame to the Chosen, for in these is a godly will that never consents to sin; the mercy of God must be knit to them, and a substance preserved in them that may never be separated from him	147
54.	We ought to rejoice that God dwelleth in our soul, and our soul in God; so that between God and our soul is nothing, but it is, as it were, all God. And how faith is ground of all power in our soul, by the Holy Ghost	150
55.	Christ is our way, leading and presenting us to the Father. And as soon as the soul is infused in the body, mercy and grace work. And how the second Person took our sensuality to save us from a double death	151
56.	It is easier to know God than our soul; for God is to us nearer. And therefore, if we will have knowing of it, we must seek into God. And he willeth that we desire to have knowledge of kind, mercy and grace	153
57.	In our substance we are full: in our sensuality we fail—which God will restore by mercy and grace. And how our kind, which is the higher part, is knit to God in the making: and God, Jesus, is knit to our kind in the lower part, in our flesh taking: and of faith spring other virtues: and Mary is our Mother	156
58.	God was never displeased with his chosen Wife; and of three properties in the Trinity, Fatherhood, Motherhood and Lordship: and how our substance is in each Person, but our sensuality is in Christ alone	158
59.	Wickedness is turned to bliss, in the chosen, by	

CONTENTS

CHAPTER		PAGE
	mercy and grace: for the property of God is to do good against ill, by Jesus, our Mother in kind grace; and the highest soul in virtue is the meekest—of which ground we have all other virtues	161
60.	How we are brought again and forthspread, by mercy and grace, of our sweet, kind and ever-loving Mother, Jesus; and of the properties of motherhood. But Jesus is our true Mother, feeding us, not with milk, but with himself: opening his side unto us, and challenging all our love	163
61.	Jesus useth more tenderness in our ghostly bringing forth: though he suffereth us to fall, for the knowing of our wretchedness, he hastily raiseth us: not breaking his love because of our trespass, for he cannot suffer his child to perish; for he willeth that we have the quality of a child, fleeing to him always in our necessity	165
62.	The love of God suffereth never his chosen to lose time: for all their trouble is turned into endless joy; and how we are all obliged to God for kindness and for grace; for every kind is in man: and we need not seek out to know various kinds, but Holy Church alone	168
63.	Sin is more painful than hell: and vile and harmful to kind; but grace saveth kind and destroyeth sin; the children of Jesus are not yet all born; they pass not the stature of childhood, but live in feebleness until they come to heaven, where joys are ever new, ever beginning, without end	169
64.	The fifteenth Revelation. The absence of God in this life is full great pain to us, apart from other travail; but we shall suddenly be taken from all pain, having Jesus for our Mother, and our patient abiding is greatly pleasing to God; and God's will is that we take our distress lightly, for love, believing ourselves always on the point of being delivered	171

CONTENTS

CHAPTER   PAGE

65. He that chooseth God, for love, with reverent meekness, is sure to be saved; which reverent meekness seeth the Lord to be marvellous great, and the self marvellous little; and it is God's will that we dread nothing but him, for the power of our enemy is locked in our Friend's hand; and therefore all that God doeth shall be of great liking to us   174

66. The sixteenth Revelation. And it is the conclusion and confirmation of all fifteen; and of her frailty and mourning in distress, and her light speaking after the great comfort of Jesus—saying that she had raved; this, being said in her great sickness, I suppose was but venial sin   176

67. Yet the Devil, after that, had great power to molest her, nigh unto death   177

68. Of the worshipful city of the soul, which is so nobly created that it might no better be made: in which the Trinity joyeth everlastingly; and the soul can have rest in nothing but in God, who sitteth therein, ruling all things   178

69. Of the Devil's second long temptation to despair   181

70. But she trusted mightily in God and in the faith of Holy Church, rehearsing to herself the passion of Christ; by which she was delivered   182

71. In all tribulation we must be steadfast in the faith, trusting mightily in God: for if our faith had no enmity it would deserve no meed; and how all these shewings are in the faith   183

72. Sin in chosen souls is deadly for a time: but they are not dead in the sight of God; and we have, here, matter for joy and mourning, because of our blindness and heaviness of the flesh; and of the most comforting look of God; and why these shewings were made   185

73. These Revelations were shown triple-wise; and of a double ghostly sureness: through which it is God's

CONTENTS

CHAPTER		PAGE
	will that we amend us, remembering his passion, knowing also that he is all love, without unreasonable heaviness for our past sins	187
74.	There are four sorts of dread; but reverent dread is a lovely, true dread that is never without meek love: yet these two are not the same; and how we should pray for them	189
75.	We need love, longing and pity; and of three sorts of longing in God, which are in us; and how, in the Day of Doom, the joy of the blessed shall be increased: seeing truly the cause of all that God hath done, trembling with awe and giving thanks with joy, marvelling at the greatness of God, and the littleness of all that is made	191
76.	A loving soul hateth sin, for its vileness, more than all the pain of hell; and how the beholding of other men's sins (except it be with compassion) hindereth the beholding of God; and the Devil, by putting into our remembrance our wretchedness, would be hindrance to the same; and of our sloth	193
77.	Of the enmity of the fiend, who loseth more in our uprising than he winneth by our falling: and therefore is he scorned; and how the scourge of God should be suffered with mind of his passion: for that is specially rewarded, above the penance chosen by ourselves; and we must needs have woe; but courteous God is our Leader, Keeper and Bliss	195
78.	Our Lord willeth that we know of four manners of goodness that he doeth to us; and how we need the light of grace to know our sin and feebleness: for we are nothing of ourselves but wretchedness; and we cannot know the horror of sin as it is; and how our enemy would that we should never know our sin until the last day: wherefore we are meekly indebted to God that sheweth it now	197
79.	We are taught concerning our own sin, and not our	

CONTENTS

CHAPTER   **PAGE**

      neighbours'—except for their help; and God willeth we know that whatsoever prompting we have contrary to this shewing cometh from our enemy; because we know the great love of God we must not be more careless about falling; and if we fall, we must hastily rise—else we are greatly unkind to God   199

80. By three things God is worshipped and we saved; and how our knowing is but an ABC: and sweet Jesus doeth all, abiding and mourning with us; but when we are in sin Christ mourneth alone: then it belongeth to us, for kindness and reverence, hastily to turn again to him   201

81. This blessed woman saw God in diverse manners: but she saw him take no resting-place but in man's soul; and he willeth that we have more enjoying in his love, than sorrowing for often falling; remembering reward everlasting, and living gladly in penance; and why God permitteth sin   202

82. God beholdeth the moaning of the soul with pity and not with blame: and yet we do naught but sin, in the which we are kept in solace and in dread; for he willeth that we turn us to him, readily cleaving to his love, and seeing that he is our medicine; and so we must love, in longing and in enjoying; and whatsoever is contrary to this is not of God but of enmity   204

83. Of three properties in God, life, love and light; and that our reason is in God, in accord: it is the highest gift; and how our faith is a light, coming of the Father, measured to us, and in this night us leading; and in the end of our woe, suddenly our eye shall be opened in full light and clarity of sight; which is our Maker, Father and Holy Ghost, in Jesus our Saviour   205

84. Charity is this light; which is not so little as not to

	merit, with labour, endless worshipful thanks of God; for faith and hope lead us to charity, which is in three manners	206
85.	God loved his chosen from without-beginning, and he never suffereth them to be hurt in a way that their bliss might be lessened; and how secrets now hid in heaven shall be known: whereof we shall bless our Lord that everything is so well ordained	207
86.	The good Lord shewed that this book should be completed otherwise than at its first writing. And he willeth that for his working we should pray thus: him thanking, trusting, and in him enjoying; and how he made this shewing because he willeth to have it known: in which knowing he will give us grace to love him: for fifteen years afterwards, it was answered that the cause of this shewing was love: which love may Jesus grant us. Amen.	208

INTRODUCTION

I

Much has been written about Julian of Norwich since her *Revelations of Divine Love* were "rediscovered" in the middle of the nineteenth century. It has been said that she was born in the East Riding of Yorkshire, between Beverley and the sea; that perhaps she came to Norwich because she married a Norfolk man—or else it was her mother, or a brother or sister, who married into a Norfolk family. Again it is said that her visions and revelations were granted to her, not at Norwich, but in her Yorkshire home; and that before becoming a recluse or anchoress (her anchorhold, it is said, was a little cell built against the wall of the Church of St Julian at Canisford, Norwich) she may have been a nun in the nearby Benedictine Convent of Carrow.

None of this information comes from Julian herself, and much of it is conjecture. Her prose and doctrine, it is true, proclaim her as belonging to the golden age of English spiritual writing. But it is the copyist of the first version of her book who tells who she was, and where and when she lived: "Here is a vision shewn by the goodness of God to a devout woman whose name is Julian. She is a recluse at Norwich and is living yet in this year of our Lord 1413."[1] There

---

[1] Cf. *A Shewing of God's Love*, the Shorter Version of *Sixteen Revelations of Divine Love* by Julian of Norwich, edited and partially modernized from the 15th-century manuscript by Sister Anna Maria Reynolds, C.P. (London, 1958), p. lviii. Sister Reynolds agrees with the previous editor of the MS. (British Museum Additional 37790), the Reverend Dundas Harford—*Comfortable words for Christ's Lovers* (London, 1911)—and with most other students of Julian, that this MS. reproduces the first "edition" of her book, and is not an abridged version of the longer text of the later MSS.

INTRODUCTION

are also bequests in a contemporary will "to Julian an anchoress at St Julian's Church, Norwich 12d. and 8d. to Sara living with her"—the date is 19 May 1404. And in Archbishop Chichele's register for 1416, there is a record of a legacy of 20 shillings to "Julian, recluse, at Norwich".

Julian herself is anxious to remain anonymous. The title she adopts for herself is the deprecatory "this creature". The sudden outburst in the Shorter Version—the only occasion on which she emphasizes her sex—"Because I am a woman, should I therefore believe that I ought not to tell you about the goodness of God, since I saw at that time that it is his will that it be known" has the appearance of an afterthought. She is warning us to pay no attention to her person—she is no teacher, but "a woman, unlettered, feeble and frail". We are to forget her, she says, "that am a wretch, . . . and behold Jesus who is teacher of all". But it occurs to her that she ought to forestall the anti-feminist objection, and say why it is that she speaks at all. It is significant that when she comes to rewrite her book, after years of reflection, she omits this identification of her sex. The reference to her mother's being amongst those who tended her in her sickness is likewise omitted from the Longer Version. She is entirely averse to our noticing her at all, except as the "creature" to whom the revelations were granted. And even then she is acutely anxious to turn our attention from herself. "I am not good", she says, "because of the shewing, but only if I love God the better. . . For if I look at myself, as a single person, I am right naught." The only occasion when she departs from this principle of not recording anything which might identify her is the allusion to St John of Beverley:

> And St John of Beverley—our Lord shewed him in his exaltation for our comfort and out of homeliness; he brought to my mind that he is a kind neighbour and of our

INTRODUCTION

knowing. And he called him St John of Beverley, just as we do.

If the words "kind neighbour" and "of our knowing" are evidence of Julian's Yorkshire origin—and this is doubtful,[1] Julian's purpose in employing them is the reverse of autobiographical. Rather she accepts the introduction of a popular English saint into the procession of saintly penitents as yet another example of God's homely dealings with his creatures—his readiness to "come down to the least part of our need".

Where Julian is deliberately and formally autobiographical is at the beginning of her second chapter:

> These Revelations were shewed to a simple unlearned creature living in this mortal flesh, in the year of our Lord one thousand three hundred and seventy-three on the thirteenth day of May.

The reason for this unwanted information is not far to seek. She is naturally at pains to establish the historicity of her Revelations. Though the place could be anywhere in England, and the "creature" any living Christian, what she tells is to be accepted as fact. Like the Great Revelation, the shewing of God's son at Bethlehem, it actually happened, it is an event in time, with a before and an after. She must solemnize her own moment of truth as the meeting-place of the eternal and the temporal, as the evangelist solemnizes the birth of the Saviour. The purpose of every authentic private revelation is to emphasize, develop and make more explicit certain aspects of the deposit of revealed truth, of the content of Christ's revelation to all—the faith which "Holy Church preacheth and teacheth". Julian repeatedly

---

[1] Cf. The Thurston–Attwater edition of Butler's *Lives of the Saints* (7 May), for the widespread cultus of John of Beverley.

insists that her own shewings and the great Revelations of the faith (of which the Church is the guardian and teacher) she "beheld as one in God's meaning". And in fact, a large part of the Longer Version of her book is devoted to the elaboration of this identity between the shewings and the faith, and the reconciliation of any apparent contradiction.

This connection between her visions and the Christian Revelation is further heightened by the emphasis she places on her own "Petrine" denial; she is as shamefaced as was Peter when the Lord turned and looked on him that she should have denied the *fact* of God's having revealed himself to her:

> I said I had raved during the day... And straightway I was sore ashamed and abashed at my recklessness... by saying I raved I shewed myself not to believe our Lord God... Alas, what a wretch I was! This was a great sin and a great unkindness...

The history of Christian spirituality is strewn with pseudo-mystics, with unconscious frauds, victims of self-delusion and what is now characterized as nervous hysteria. The Church and those saints who have been the recipients of genuine mystical experience have always been alive to the possibility of illusion. Julian's contemporary, Margery Kempe, was almost obsessed with anxiety as to whether it was God or the Devil who "wrought in her soul", and in fact she sought out Julian for assurance on this point. Walter Hilton in the *Scale of Perfection* offers advice on distinguishing true and false "illuminations", and speaks at length of how easily one may be deceived on the subject of imaginative visions. Julian is fully alive to the problem; and to solve it, she is forced to reveal herself. In the interests of the truth she scrutinizes her own behaviour and reactions, physical and psychological, before, during and after her revelations;

and this with a lucidity and exactness such as would do credit to a trained psychologist. She desired a sickness unto death for its purifying and detaching qualities, the perspective which it can give to purely human values; the sanity of her approach to the problem robs this desire of hers of the seeming-bizarre. In the course of her sickness she records all the physical changes in her condition with a clinical detachment, as well as the effects that sickness and pain may have on the interior life and its phases of consolation and desolation. She notes also the reactions of the persons attending her, particularly of the priest to whom she confides her doubts—and in recording her reflections on his reactions, she observes how physical suffering is a partial cause of the lessening of her faith.

Julian, who yields place to none in her expressions of tender affection for the person of our Lord, is even more remarkable in her gift for detached self-analysis, even under great stress. Amongst her more vivid descriptive passages is her account of a nightmare-vision of the Devil. She suddenly awakes to the smell of smoke and the feeling of great heat; though her immediate reaction is to believe that the place is on fire, there is none of that feverish panic which would be normal in one who is at the crisis of a serious illness. Again in recording her psycho-physical reactions under a severe temptation to despair, we are given an astonishing glimpse of wry humour;

> I thought to myself: "Thou hast now great earnestness about keeping thee in the faith, that thou shouldst not be taken by thine enemies. If now from this time thou shouldst ever more be as busy about keeping thee from sin, this would be a good and sovereign occupation."

This same gift of detached observation is most apparent in the descriptions of what she calls her "bodily sights"—her

INTRODUCTION

imaginative visions of our Lord on the Cross. Before ever she says what she feels, she sets down with calm and deliberate detail what it is she sees. It has often been suggested that her descriptions reflect contemporary art and the devotional literature of the period; but in fact they challenge all comparison. There is nothing in painting or pulpit literature to match her sketch of the bleeding of the Sacred Head—of the two garlands one upon the other—or of the changing colour in the face of the dying Christ. It is noteworthy that her own unique comparison is with the allegedly miraculous vernicle—the imprint of Christ's face on the towel of Veronica—where the point of the comparison is precisely that the picture is alive with movement and change of colour. She has much to say of the sufferings caused by the physical thirst of Christ and by the loss of moisture in his crucified body. The medical descriptions based on the Holy Shroud of Turin or the precise reconstructions of Scripture-scholars from the text of the Gospels are lifeless alongside Julian's. Nor is her exact image of the cloth hanging out to dry one that springs readily to our minds when we examine a medieval crucifix. One may, of course, explain all by crediting her with an imagination unequalled by any artistic expression of her period. But we would go beyond the evidence if we asserted that her imagination is diseased or disordered.

In the great parabolic allegory of the Lord and the Servant, she is at pains to distinguish exactly the various kinds of vision of which it is constructed;[1] she itemizes with scrupulous care the physical characteristics of the figures of the allegory, and afterwards relates the parabolic meaning of each detail. She has an eye for detail—and it is the synthetic eye of the expert photographer. But we feel that it is

[1] For an exact analysis of the types of Julian's visions, cf. Paul Molinari, S.J., *Julian of Norwich* (London, 1958), pp. 32–48.

not in her, not even unconsciously, to "fake" details or to distort the focus. She records what she sees.

Given such insight as this into the character of the author, the absence of specific biographical detail in the *Revelations* becomes comparatively unimportant. Alongside Julian, the author of the *Cloud of Unknowing* and even Walter Hilton are dim figures of the past. The spiritual teaching, and indeed the whole of her mystical theology, is embedded in the strong framework of this highly personal writing. There is, of course, a good deal of the traditional "spiritual biography" to be found in it. We can isolate the elements of the *ascensio mentis in Deum*, and show how they conform to the already traditional pattern of Purgation, Illumination and Union.[1] We may point out that her desire for a sickness is a form of the "second conversion", and the sickness itself was a definitive purification—the fulfilment of her desire "to be purified; so as afterwards to live more according to the worship of God". We may even say that in the three days and three nights of her sickness, "being made perfect in a short space, she fulfilled a long time", she passed rapidly through all the successive stages of infused prayer which we find listed in the manuals of mystical theology, as far as the rarefied heights of the mystical marriage; and that thereafter she lived more or less constantly in the state of the transforming union. Yet all this involves much inference, and a certain anachronism in the use of terminology. She pays as little heed in her teaching to the degrees of the spiritual life, as God himself paid little heed to them in the graces which he gave to her. All her infused graces she received during the time of her purification. And we cannot be sure that she had any further mystical experience in the strictest sense, after her "triduum" in 1373, except the answer she received fifteen or more years later when she "was answered in

[1] Cf. Molinari, *op. cit.*, Part II *passim*.

INTRODUCTION

ghostly understanding" that "love was his meaning", and the further inward teaching, after twenty years, on the meaning of the parable of the Lord and the Servant. It is true that afterwards the whole of the Revelation was often brought "liberally to the sight of my understanding"; but we have no means of judging whether the shewings recurred according to the identical mystical pattern of direct infusion, or whether, with the assistance of "ordinary" actual graces, she recalled them in the imaginative and conceptual dress with which she first covered them. And though the frequent "lightings and touchings", by which she received further understanding on the shewings, indicate that she was often the recipient of infused graces, we cannot conclude that the transforming union was in any way her habitual state.

Similarly, her teaching on prayer is not presented as the fruit of a gradual experience over the years, but as the direct result of the fourteenth revelation—"our Lord shewed me concerning prayer", and of part of the first, where again she "saw" concerning prayer. Again, we may be sure that ever after she would pray as she "was learned", as she had seen; and it is reasonable to suppose that her prayer would be frequently, if not habitually, contemplative. But this, too, is inference, not autobiography.

We may perhaps infer that Julian, in speaking of "seeing" our Lord—the manhood with the Godhead—dwelling in her soul, is actually enjoying the transforming union. Yet she is not describing, as a Teresa or John of the Cross describes, her own conscious experience of this union, but rather what is going on in every soul in grace—that dynamic union which is the essence of the supernatural life.[1] Julian's divinely imposed task is *contemplata tradere*. This is her only interest in recounting her mystical experience. For the rest "seeking is as good as beholding", and whether the Lord

[1] Cf. Molinari, *op. cit.*, pp. 163–4.

INTRODUCTION

gives the finding here or hereafter is all one, as long as "we seek busily and without sloth". To this end, in the Longer Version at least, she avoids all mention of the words "contemplation" and "contemplative".[1] She is not writing specifically for religious, much less for recluses, but for all God's lovers, all her "even-christians" who find in their hearts this love-longing.

Hence, even as a traditional spiritual biography, Julian's book retains its emphatic individuality. She is bent on giving, not an account of her own interior life, but what she believed God to have shewed, and how his shewings are to be compounded with that teaching which belongs to us all as "seekers"—the faith of Holy Church. We know her then, when we meet her in the pages of Margery Kempe. We recognize her in her judgement, her detachment, the strength of her decisiveness. She is the expert in good counsel, who applies to Margery's problem not only the gift of discernment which is so apparent in her book, but her deep knowledge of scripture and of the Fathers—the faith, the traditional teaching of the Church. But above all we recognize her in the exquisite charity she shews to one who, to say the least of it, cuts a quaint figure, and must have been a staple subject for unpleasant gossip in Julian's Norwich. We feel about Julian as Julian felt about John of Beverley when God shewed him—that she is "a kind neighbour and of our knowing".

---

[1] There is one exception, which in itself is most significant: "In this I taught that though we be lifted high in contemplation by the special gift of our Lord yet it behoveth us therewith to have sight of our sin and of our feebleness. For without this knowing we cannot be safe" (c.78, p. 203).
Julian here speaks of high contemplation simply as an hypothesis, in order to stress the point she wishes to make.

INTRODUCTION

II

Julian's own assertion in the first version of her *Revelations*, that she is no teacher, "but a woman unlettered, feeble and frail",[1] has doubtless been taken too literally. The title of the third edition of the Amherst MS., *Comfortable Words for Christ's Lovers*,[2] is perhaps indicative of the attitude even of Julian's most fervent admirers.[3] The value of her *Revelations*, it would seem, is devotional, not theological; and it lies in her successful communication of her experience of the tender love of God and her own childlike trust. Her appeal is to the heart, not to the head. The theologian admirer of Julian will insist that she is not writing a theological treatise, and that when she speaks on matters which require theological *expertise*, she is likely to be obscure and, it may be, erroneous, precisely because she is speaking outside her brief. She is spokesman not for theologians, but for the fervent and not very learned: for those who know, but do not know why or how they know, and are not concerned with the why and the how.

Hence, though she is always mentioned in the company of the great fourteenth-century English spiritual writers, Hilton and the author of the *Cloud of Unknowing*, she is inclined to be treated as a poor relation. Students of Middle English literature have spoken of the high quality of her prose, but never more than in very general terms, or in passing.[4] A version of her book was already in print before the end of the seventeenth century, but her own text is still

---

[1] Reynolds, *op. cit.*, p. 17.   [2] Dundas Harford, London, 1925.

[3] Fr Molinari's book is the first serious and sustained attempt at a theological evaluation of the *Revelations*. He limits himself to a discussion of the authenticity of the shewings, and of Julian's teaching on prayer.

[2] Cf. Reynolds, *op. cit.*, pp. xxii ff. for a brief but illuminating discussion of Julian's prose style.

INTRODUCTION

unavailable. It may well be that her qualities as a writer of English prose have been neglected partly because the content of the *Revelations* has never been considered, by the historian of Spiritual Theology, to be more than second class and amateur. But though she never attended the schools of Oxford or Paris with Hilton and the author of the *Cloud*, she does speak their language, in every sense. There is little to choose, for example, on the point of doctrine, between the ascesis of the strongly Dionysian *Epistle of Privy Counselling*, and that of c. 5 of the *Revelations*:

> ... strip, spoil, and utterly unclothe thyself of all manner of feeling of thyself, that thou mayest be able to be clothed with the gracious feeling of God himself. And this is the true condition of a perfect lover, only and utterly to spoil himself for that thing that he loveth, and not admit nor suffer to be clothed but only in that thing that he loveth...[1] He is our clothing that, for love, wrappeth us up and windeth us about... We need to have knowledge of this—that we should reckon as naught everything that is made, to love and have God who is unmade... When the soul is willingly naughted, for love, so as to have him who is all, then is she able to receive ghostly rest.

Walter Hilton, in his teaching on contemplative prayer, is at pains to emphasize the Christological approach of the traditional spirituality, particularly in the use of his sources.[2] In this he is at one with the author of the *Cloud*, who makes much of the Johannine symbol of Christ as the door to the Godhead.[3] So Hilton will say, at the end of the *Scale of Per-*

---

[1] *The Cloud of Unknowing and Other Treatises*, ed. McCann (London, 1952), p. 122.

[2] Cf. *The Goad of Love*, ed. Kirchberger (Faber and Faber, London, 1952), pp. 24–6.

[3] McCann, *op. cit.*, pp. 123–5. It is perhaps worth remarking that

INTRODUCTION

fection (Book II): ". . . when I say that grace worketh I mean love, Jesus, and God: for all is one and naught but one."[1] Julian, who "saw in Christ that the Father is", begins here. In her account of the first shewing she says: "The Trinity is our endless joy and our bliss, by our Lord Jesus Christ and in our Lord Jesus Christ. And this was shewed in the first sight and in them all. For where Jesus appeareth the blessed Trinity is understood." Nor does this prevent her from entering "within the ghostly door". She sees, with the same clarity as the author of the *Cloud* (or as Ruysbroeck) that "the making of many means" is not the highest prayer:

> . . . because of unknowing of love, we employ many means. Then I saw truly that it is greater worship to God, and truly more delightful to him, if we pray to himself and of his goodness, and cleave thereunto, by his grace, with true understanding and steadfast belief, than if we used all the means that heart can think.[2]

Of her sight of the Divine Indwelling, Julian writes:

> And thus I understood truly that our soul may never have rest in anything that is beneath itself. And when it cometh above all creatures into itself, yet it cannot dwell in the beholding of itself; but all its beholding is blissfully set in God who is the Maker, dwelling therein (c.68).

This passage implies a thorough acquaintance with the

---

the immediate source of the *Cloud's* Dionysianism is the Victorine Thomas Gallus, the founder of the school, who did not hesitate to write, in his short treatise on the name of Jesus: "In the single name of Jesus the whole structure of religion and all the canons of holiness are contained."

[1] Ed. Underhill (London, 1923), pp. 441-2.

[2] C.6. We may note that amongst these "means" Julian lists his holy flesh, holy passion, holy cross, etc.

Augustinian *ascensio mentis in Deum* and the doctrine of the re-formation of the soul according to the image of God, with which Hilton deals at such length, particularly in *Scale* II:

> Nevertheless I say not that thy soul shall rest still in this knowing [*sc.* of itself], but it shall by this seek higher knowing above itself, and that is, the kind of God. For thy soul is but a mirror, in the which thou shalt see God ghostly.[1]

Julian seems to have known the *Stimulus Amoris* of James of Milan, which Hilton translated and adapted for English readers, under the title of *The Goad of Love*. The effect of sin, she says, is to "befoul the fair image of God" (c.39). Hilton says that the contrite soul sees "his fair image so blacked", and that sin has "made foul the image".[2] The same doctrine is very much in evidence in Julian's account of the shewing of the face of the dying Christ (c.10). One of the key texts in the traditional exposé of this doctrine is II Corinthians 3.18: "nos vero omnes, revelata facie, gloriam Domini speculantes, in eandem imaginem transformamur."[3] Julian's allusion to this text is unmistakable:

> This was a delightful sight [*sc.* the Indwelling] and a restful shewing, that is without end. And the beholding of this, while we are here, is full pleasant to God and full

---

[1] Underhill, *op. cit.*, pp. 357–8. Cf. also p. 96.

[2] Kirchberger, *op. cit.*, pp. 135, 185. The Editor, in a note on the word "blacked", wonders if "Hilton is thinking of the visual image in Julian's *Revelations*" (c.10). It does not seem possible to date with any accuracy Hilton's various writings (or those of the author of the *Cloud*). The Longer Version of the *Revelations* was certainly not written before 1395. We know that Margery Kempe had Hilton's version of the *Stimulus* read to her; it is reasonable to presume that Julian knew it.

[3] "But we all beholding the glory of the Lord with open face, are transformed into the same image."

INTRODUCTION

great speed to us. And the soul that thus beholdeth—the sight maketh it like to him that is beheld, and oneth it to him in rest and in peace, by his grace (c.68).

It is in a similar context that the author of the *Cloud* interprets the Psalmist's "Lord, the light of thy face is stamped upon us" as follows: "The light of God's face is the shining of his grace, that reformeth in us his image."[1] The highest and best part of contemplation, he says, is for a man to "have God continuously dwelling in him, and live in love and in sight of the high peace of the Godhead."[2] When the same author wishes to stress the supreme importance of the work of contemplation—Julian's seeking and beholding—for the well-being of the Church, he says:

> For as all men were lost in Adam, because he fell from this oneing affection, and as all . . . be saved and shall be by the virtue of the passion of Christ alone, offering himself up in the veriest sacrifice, all that he was in general and not in special, without special beholding to any one man in this life, but generally and in common for all: right so a very and a perfect sacrificer of himself, thus by a common intent unto all, doth that in him is to knit all men to God as effectually as himself is.[3]

Much of this summarizes what Julian perceived in the Parable of the Lord and the Servant—the hinge of all the teaching of the *Revelations*. Julian shares with Hilton and the author of the *Cloud* a common spiritual heritage. What they have assimilated through the study of Holy Scripture, the Fathers and theologians, is revealed to her in the shewings.

---

[1] *Deonise Hid Divinite*, ed. Hodgson (Early English Text Society, London, 1955). The quotation is taken from the author's adaptation of Richard of St Victor's *Beniamin Minor* (p. 44).

[2] *Ibid.* (from *A Tretis of Discrecyon of Spirites*), p. 85.

[3] McCann, *op. cit.*, p. 109. And cf. also pp. 41–2.

They all dilate on the main themes of the traditional spirituality—the second conversion, humility and charity as the twin pillars of the spiritual edifice, the "lively" desire for God as the primary motive, the fact that any kind of agitation, wrath, unpeace, frowardness, proceeds from blindness and unknowing, and is the main obstacle to spiritual growth.[1] They also share a common spiritual terminology. The very words which are picked out as the characteristic language of Julian's devotional approach, "homely", "courtesy", "compassion", belong as well to the theologians. Most of their treatises were written for purposes of spiritual direction. And we learn from the *Book of Margery Kempe* that Julian performed the same function:

> Then she was bidden by our Lord to go to an anchoress in the same city, named Dame Jelyan, and so she did, and showed her the grace that God put into her soul, of compunction, contrition, sweetness and devotion, compassion with holy meditation and high contemplation, and full many holy speeches and dalliance that our Lord spake to her soul; and many wonderful revelations, which she shewed to the anchoress to find out if there were any deceit in them, for the anchoress was expert in such things, and good counsel could give.
>
> The anchoress, hearing the marvellous goodness of our Lord, highly thanked God with all her heart for his visitation, counselling this creature to be obedient to the will of our Lord God and to fulfil with all her might whatever he put into her soul, if it were not against the worship of God, and profit of her fellow Christians, for if it were, then it were not the moving of a good spirit, but

---

[1] "For whoso lacketh peace and restfulness of heart, him lacketh the lively presence of the lovely sight of the high peace of heaven, good gracious God, his own dear self" (Hodgson, *op. cit.*, p. 84). Cf. *Revelations*, cc. 10, 47, 52, 72, etc.

rather of an evil spirit. "The Holy Ghost moveth ne'er a thing against charity, for if he did, he would be contrary to his own self, for he is all charity. Also he moveth a soul to all chasteness, for chaste livers are called the Temple of the Holy Ghost, and the Holy Ghost maketh a soul stable and steadfast in the right faith, and the right belief.

And a double man in soul is ever unstable and unsteadfast in all his ways. He that is ever doubting is like the flood of the sea which is moved and borne about with the wind, and that man is not likely to receive the gifts of God.

Any creature that hath these tokens may steadfastly believe that the Holy Ghost dwelleth in his soul. And much more when God visiteth a creature with tears of contrition, devotion and compassion, he may and ought to believe that the Holy Ghost is in his soul. Saint Paul saith that the Holy Ghost asketh for us with mourning and weeping unspeakable, that is to say, he maketh us to ask and pray with mourning and weeping so plenteously that the tears may not be numbered. No evil spirit may give these tokens, for Saint Jerome saith that tears torment more the devil than do the pains of Hell. God and the devil are ever at odds and they shall never dwell together in one place, and the devil hath no power in a man's soul.

Holy Writ saith that the soul of a rightful man is the seat of God, and so I trust, sister, that ye be. I pray God grant you perseverance."[1]

Learning, lucidity, assurance, decision. All the marks of the competent spiritual director are portrayed here, one well-

---

[1] *The Book of Margery Kempe*: A Modern Version, ed. W. Butler-Bowdon (Jonathan Cape, 1940), pp. 72–4.

versed in the discernment of spirits. Julian, if we may trust Margery, loses nothing in a comparison with the author of the *Cloud*, in the following passage from his *Pistle of Discrecioun of Stirings*:

> And perhaps thou knowest not yet thine own inward disposition thyself as fully as thou shalt do hereafter, when God will let thee feel it by the proof, among many fallings and risings. For I knew never yet a sinner who could come to the perfect knowing of himself and his inward dispositions, unless he were learned of it before, in the school of God, by experience of many temptations. For right as among the waves and the floods and the storms of the sea, on the one part, and the peaceable wind and the calms and the soft weather on the other part, the silly ship at the last attaineth to the land and the haven: right so among the diversity of temptations and tribulations that fall to a soul in this ebbing and flowing life . . . and among the grace and the goodness of the Holy Ghost, the manifold visitations, sweetness and comfort of the spirit . . . the silly soul . . . attaineth at the last to the land of stableness and the haven of help, the which is the clear and soothfast knowing of himself and of all his inward dispositions.[1]

III

It may be argued, then, that as a spiritual teacher Julian is of the same calibre as her more celebrated contemporaries. Like theirs, her theme is the loving relationship between God and the souls of the just. "Thus was I learned that love is our Lord's meaning. And I saw full surely in this, and in all, that before God made us, he loved us. Which love was never slaked, nor ever shall be. And in this love he hath done all

[1] Hodgson, *op. cit.*, p. 64.

his works. And in this love he hath made all things profitable to us. And in this love our life is everlasting. In our making we had beginning: but the love wherein he made us was in him from without-beginning. In which love we have our beginning. And all this shall we see in God without end." These closing words of the *Revelations* are a synopsis of the whole book; its title might well have been "A Treatise of the Divine Love".

At first sight, however, the only shape and rhythm which her book seems to have is chronological: the apparently haphazard and arbitrary order of the shewings themselves. But a closer examination reveals that she has found therein what turns out to be a highly logical and artistic structure. In the first place, the shewings are the answer to her prayer ". . . to receive three wounds in my life; that is to say, the wound of true contrition, the wound of kind compassion, and the wound of earnest longing for God" (c.2). The first eleven revelations manifest, progressively, an ever deeper insight into the meaning of "suffering with" the crucified Christ: the answer to the Pauline prayer, "Him I would learn to know, and the virtue of his resurrection, and what it means to share his sufferings, moulded into the pattern of his death."[1]

The first part of the *Revelations* (cc.1–26), the great shewings of the dying Christ, with their interstices and the concluding shewing of Christ glorified, focus themselves around, and develop, the crucial Pauline text on the meaning of the interior life: "My old self has become dead to the law that I may live to God; with Christ I hang upon the Cross, and yet I am alive; or rather not I; it is Christ that lives in me. True, I am living, here and now, this mortal life; but my real life is my faith in the Son of God, who loved me and gave himself for me."[2] To understand

[1] Philippians 3. 10. [2] Galatians 2. 20.

"God's kindly will to have us" demands a living knowledge of the union between God and man, of the hypostatic union, of the Blessed Trinity working in "our making and again-making", and of the accomplishment of this working in time and eternity. This knowledge is wisdom and truth.

So Julian is shewn, first, the suffering Christ, and then the wisdom and truth in the soul of her who has received the gift, those wounds of kind compassion and earnest longing; she is shewn the Trinity in the suffering Christ as Maker, Lover and Keeper; she sees why she must long with all her strength for God, and that the expression of this longing is "the highest prayer"—the reflection of God's own ineffable longing for the soul of his choice; she sees that there is a hindrance in us to the progressive fulfilment of this longing, but that Christ's stooping and suffering and our seeking remove the hindrance; and she is shewn that there is no power outside us which can stand against the divine power generated in God's chosen by his stooping and suffering; she is taught in the word of Christ, "Art thou well paid that ever suffered I passion for thee?", that love of Christ which passes all knowledge, and the joy and bliss which God's fullness confers.[1] So she propounds her thesis —the eternal demonstration of the Power, Wisdom and Love which is Divine Providence. As she saw Christ's Mother in the first shewing, so now she sees her again at the end of this first part—the theory, as it were, in practice: ". . . wilt thou see how I love her so that thou mightest joy with me in the love that I have in her, and she in me? . . . Wilt thou see in her how thou art loved?" (c.25). And finally Julian is shewn Christ glorified, and sees that "In Christ the whole plenitude of Deity is embodied, and dwells in him, and it is in him that you find your completion; he is

[1] Cf. Ephesians 3. 18.

INTRODUCTION

the fountain head from which all dominion and power proceed."[1]

The great objection to this thesis of the fulfilment of the Trinitarian Providence in Christ—"I it am that is all", of the Eternal Wisdom that "reacheth from end to end mightily, and ordereth all things sweetly",[2] is sin. The divine longing is to be fulfilled in the longing of his chosen: but she beholds "in us all in general" that sin is the hindrance (c.27). She has already noticed that our again-making through the pains of Christ is integral to the divine plan of love, and that it consists in the reconciliation of the outward part of our nature, "which is now in pain and woe [because of sin] and shall be, in this life", with the inward part, which "is a high and blessed life which is all in peace and love" (c.19). This conflict forces itself on her attention specifically in c.27; and it is not too much to say that the elucidation of the problem, in its various aspects, imparts an essential structure to the rest of her book.

Towards the end of the *Revelations*, when she is speaking of Christ who performs all the works unto salvation in us from first to last, for all these works are his, Julian adds: "I believe and understand the ministrations of Holy Angels, as theologians tell; but this was not shewed to me. For himself is nearest and meekest, highest and lowest, and doeth all..." One of these theologians is Walter Hilton,[3] in his *Scale* II, where he says, speaking of the soul reformed in faith and feeling:

---

[1] Colossians 2. 9–10. Cf. "I it am, I it am", etc. (c.26). We may note that the eleventh and twelfth shewings make a perfect *inclusio* with the first shewing.   [2] Wisdom 8. 1.

[3] Another is the author of the *Cloud*, telling of the "Ghostly wisdom in very contemplation and high savour of the Godhead". "And all this shall be done suddenly, listily and graciously, without business or travail of thyself, only by the ministration of the angels through the virtue of this lovely blind work" (McCann, *op. cit.* pp. 111–12). This theory of angelic mediation is, of course, Dionysian in origin.

INTRODUCTION

> It may not be told by tongue the feelings, the lightenings, the graces and the comforts in special, that clean souls perceive through favourable fellowship of blessed angels... But then with the help of angels, yet the soul seeth more. For knowing riseth above this in a clean soul; and that is to behold the blessed kind of Jesus. First of his glorious manhood, how it is worthily highed above all angels' kind; and then after of his blessed Godhead, for by knowing of creatures is known the Creator. And then beginneth the soul for to perceive a little of the privities of the blessed Trinity... then it is opened soothfastly to the eyes of the soul the onehead in substance and distinction of persons in the blessed Trinity, as it may be seen here, and mickle other soothfastness of this blessed Trinity.[1]

But it is St John of the Cross who describes more exactly the content of the *Revelations*, in his account of the knowledge granted to the soul in the transforming union:

> "And then we shall go forth To the lofty caverns of the rock"... The rock of which she here speaks, according to S. Paul, is Christ. The lofty caverns of the rock are the lofty and high and deep mysteries of the wisdom of God which are in Christ, concerning the hypostatical union of human nature with the Divine Word, and the correspondence to this which is the union of men in God, and in the agreement which there is between the justice and the mercy of God as to the salvation of the human race in the manifestation of his judgements.[2]

---

[1] Underhill, *op. cit.*, pp. 461–2. Hilton here seems to be following the scheme of Richard of St Victor's *ascensio mentis in Deum* as propounded in the *Beniamin Maior* and the *De Trinitate*.

[2] *The Spiritual Canticle*, ed. Allison Peers (London, 1934), Vol. II, p. 385. This going forth is the entry of the Bride "farther into the Spiritual Marriage".

INTRODUCTION

These passages enable us to see more precisely the structure of the *Revelations*. Julian insists again and again that she saw only those that shall be saved—"God shewed me none other". She did not see clearly or directly "the agreement which there is between the justice and the mercy of God as to the salvation of the human race".[1] Hence, between the first twelve shewings and the sixteenth, itself a separate "entry into the cavern",[2] Julian twice beseeches our Lord for further enlightenment; and is answered each time by a "leading of the understanding"; each time the original thesis is repeated, with progressive enlightenment and additional teaching "concerning the hypostatical union . . . and the union of men [for Julian, "those that shall be saved"] in God".

In this second going forth (c. 27), she observes, first, that sin is known only by the pain and sorrow; and that these effects are covered and remedied by the compassion of Christ, as has been shewn; so that the anguish and the tribulation of the Church ("all that shall be saved") is, *sub specie aeternitatis*, a thing of joy and bliss; and further, that these effects of sin, through his compassion, work a purification in us. But still the limited nature of her vision causes her to say "but how can all be well in face of the great harm that is come by sin to thy creatures?" (c. 29). The immediate answer is that the great remedy found by the blessed Trinity for Adam's sin is a sure token that the same Power can and will make lesser things well: that and the fact that it belongs to the union of wills not to seek to know the secret of the king—"all that belongeth not to our salvation". But it is re-

[1] Hilton indicates that this special knowledge of ghostly things will extend to a knowledge of the reproved: "how rightfully he forsaketh them and leaveth them in their sin and doth them no wrong; how he rewardeth them in this world, suffering them for to have fulfilling of their will, and after this for to punish them endlessly" (Underhill, *op. cit.*, p. 456). Julian is shewn nothing of this.

[2] The shewing of the Divine Indwelling in c. 68.

vealed that in the oneing of all mankind with the blessed Trinity at the last day "thou shalt see thyself that all manner of things shall be well" (c.31). Julian again voices her misgiving: the Church teaches that the wicked angels and those that die out of charity will be damned eternally. "In view of all this it seemed to me impossible that all manner of things should be well according as our Lord shewed in this time. But I had no other answer to the difficulty in this shewing of our Lord's except this: 'What is impossible to thee is not impossible to me; I shall save my word in all things—I shall make all things well'" (c. 32). It has been suggested that Julian, at least in her way of speaking, is here suspect of Origenism; that she hints that this great deed which the Trinity shall do to make all well at the last will be the conversion of the "reproved". But this is to forget the advice of the scribe of the Paris MS.: "And beware that thou take not one thing and leave another, according to thy affection and liking—for that is the way of an heretic, but take everything with other." Julian has already seen, in the third shewing, the scorning of the Devil (c.13); and in the present context (c.33) she is shewn that this scorning, *sc.* eternal damnation, extends to all the Devil's sort. Within her own terms of reference she succeeds in shewing that the final solution does belong to the moment of "the completed growth of Christ",[1] when his ghostly thirst shall have an end; it is a knowledge which belongs to the confirmation in grace of the whole body, to the *beata pacis visio*, to surety in deed, not in hope.[2] These chapters are a lucid and illuminating commentary on the words "and the gates of Hell shall

[1] Ephesians 4. 13.

[2] Julian tells us, obliquely, why our Lord never shewed her the "reproved": "Whenever in our folly we turn to behold the reproved, tenderly our Lord toucheth us and blissfully claspeth, saying in our soul: 'Let be, my love, my most dear child, and attend to me (for I am enough to thee), and take joy in thy Saviour and thy salvation'" (c.36).

never prevail". What is remarkable here is not the limpet-like nature of Julian's blind faith, but what she *sees* the Church to be:

> God shewed the very great pleasure that he taketh in all men and women who mightily and wisely receive the preaching and teaching of Holy Church. For he is Holy Church. He is its ground. He is its substance. He is its teaching. He is its teacher. He is the end and the reward towards which every kind soul travelleth. This is known and shall be known to every soul to whom the Holy Ghost declareth it. And indeed I hope that all those who so seek shall speed; for they seek God (c.34).

In this section occur two of the most controversial chapters in her book (37–8). They tempt the average theologian to dismiss her as unsound. In the first she is shewn that she will sin, but God says "I keep thee full surely". She sees that "in every soul that shall be saved is a godly will that never assenteth to sin and never shall. Just as there is a beastly will in the lower part which can will nothing good, so there is a godly will in the higher part, a will so good that it can never will evil but ever willeth the good." And in the second she says: "God shewed that sin shall be no shame but rather worship for man. . . The soul that shall come to heaven is so precious to God, and the place itself is so worshipful, that the goodness of God never permitteth a soul that is to come thither to sin."[1] Even Julian's champions are uncomfortable, and offer her statement in c.40:

> But if now, because of all this comfort that I have mentioned, any man or woman is foolishly tempted to say or think that if this is true, it must be good to sin in order to

---

[1] The Paris MS. here reads "sin finally", as against the Sloane MSS. "sin". This seems an obvious case of the *lectio difficilior potior*, even though the context shews that "sin finally" is the obvious meaning.

INTRODUCTION

have a greater reward, or else to attach less weight to sinning—let them beware of this temptation,

as a sort of retraction. Julian's context here, of course, is not that of the moral or dogmatic theologian. She is primarily speaking of and for those whose approach is her own: whose staple food is the kind of unitive prayer of which she speaks at length at the end of this section (cc.41–3): the contemplative prayer of seeking, thanking and—where the grace is given—beholding. It is for such souls that she defines the prayer of beseeching as "a true and grace-giving, lasting will of the soul which is oned and fastened to the will of our Lord, by the sweet and secret working of the Holy Ghost" (c.41). This is none other than the traditional *castissima oratio* of the contemplative, the extension or the raising of the mind and the heart. It is, in the words of the author of the *Cloud*, ". . . this sweet subtle working, the which in itself is the high wisdom of the Godhead graciously descending into man's soul, knitting it and oneing it to himself in ghostly subtlety and prudence of spirit".[1] Though she seems anxious throughout the *Revelations* to avoid giving the impression that she is writing a treatise for contemplatives, there is no mistaking her conviction that the vigour of the Body of Christ depends on those who earnestly desire to live unto God and who must, therefore, seek busily and pray inwardly. Though, again, she is not concerned to distinguish rigidly between the various stages and levels of the spiritual life, her thought and language in these apparently unorthodox chapters obviously refer us to the contemplative purification,[2] to the second conversion, and to that

---

[1] McCann, *op. cit.*, p. 112.

[2] Like Hilton and the author of the *Cloud*, she is a "moderate" on the subject of voluntary mortification, and she points out that true compassion involves the willing acceptance of desolation—and that this very definitely includes the dreadful sense of sin and guilt which is part of the contemplative purification.

INTRODUCTION

malaise of soul in which the consciousness of the least deliberate sin brings with it a bitterness akin to despair.[1] Hence the statement of c.40, cited above, is in no way a retraction, nor an admission of having written obscurely. It is a *caveat* to the reader who may not be of like mind with herself, who may not be convinced that "Sin is the sharpest scourge that any chosen soul can be smitten with—a scourge which greatly afflicteth a man or woman, breaketh him in pieces and purgeth him of his self-love; to the extent that at times he thinketh himself fit for nothing but to sink into hell" (c.39). It is for such a soul that she elaborates her teaching in this chapter in the last part of her book—the chapters on doubtful dread. We may also note, *à propos* the great penitents of c.38, that the joy and honour is for the willing acceptance of the sorrow and shame which are the effects of sin. It is also by no means certain that she is speaking specifically of grave sin, in the theological sense. For whatever is to be said of the sin of St Peter, it has surely never been a common theological opinion that Thomas's doubting was a grave sin. What she is stressing is that these high saints are models of penitence; and that their sins, like that of Adam, may be counted as *felices culpae*, because of the effect of the remedy in them. The passage is, in fact, a com-

[1] It is perhaps worth while to recall here the annotation which precedes the exposition of the first stanza of the *Spiritual Canticle* of St John of the Cross: "The soul, taking account of her obligations . . . knowing that he has created her for himself alone for which she owes him all the rest of the love of her will, and the return of his love to her . . . in order to remedy so much evil and harm, especially as she sees God to be very far distant and hidden, since she has been content to forget him so much among creatures, she is touched with fear and inward grief of heart at so great perdition and peril, and renounces all things, ceases from all business, and delays not a day neither an hour. Then, with yearning and sighs that come from the heart, wounded now with love for God, she begins to invoke her beloved . . ." (a classic text on the subject of the second conversion. Allison Peers, *loc. cit.*, pp. 186–7).

ment on the text: "There shall be joy before the angels of God upon one sinner that doth penance, more than upon ninety-nine just who need not penance."[1] We must bear in mind, as well, that Julian's fundamental treatment of these difficulties is not here, but in the third part of her book (cc.44–65), which is built round the all-important Parable of the Lord and the Servant. This parable is the focal point of the *Revelations*; it represents her third going forth into the lofty caverns, "the marvellous high deepness" of the divine wisdom. Julian is most widely known, I suppose, for the beauties of her teaching on the Motherhood of Christ. But this doctrine is, at best, only half-understood—it remains a mere metaphor—except in the light and the meaning of this parable. Julian's anthropology[2] is entirely dependent on it.

During the time of the shewings of the dying Christ, when her prayer "I would that his pains were my pains" was being answered, Julian had observed that she felt within herself a regret for having so prayed: "Had I known what it was like, I would have been loath to pray for it." "This", she said, "was merely the grumbling and frailty of the flesh without consent of the soul, to which God assigneth no blame." And she draws a distinction between the outward part of our nature, "our mortal flesh which is now in pain and woe", and the inward part, "a high and a blessed life which is all in peace and in love". She saw also that the inward part is master, and that it pays no heed to the clamourings of the flesh, "but all the intent of the will is set endlessly to be oned to our Lord Jesus"; and again, "that the outward part could draw the inward to its own assent—this was not shewed to me; but that the inward part, by grace, draweth the outward part,

---

[1] Luke 15. 7.
[2] I use this word in the sense in which the Greek Fathers used it—the science of the nature of man in his relationship to God.

INTRODUCTION

and both shall be oned in bliss without end by the power of Christ—this was shewed" (c.19).

This passage serves as an introduction to the third part (cc. 44–65) in which Julian develops her anthropology. It emphasizes that she is never speaking of the nature of man in the abstract, but always of those that shall be saved in Christ: of those who are already (to use Hilton's terminology) reformed and kept in the faith, and are in process of being reformed in feeling—by the power of Christ. Julian takes for granted an acquaintance with Augustinian psychology—in some such simplified form as is found in Hilton's *Scale* II:

> For thou shalt understand that a soul hath two parts. The one is called the sensuality; that is the fleshly feeling by the outward wits, the which is common to man and beast. Of the which sensuality, when it is unreasonably and inordinately ruled, is made the image of sin... For then is the sensuality sin, when it is not ruled after reason. The other part is called reason, and that is departed in two: in the over part, and in the nether part. The over part is likened to a man, for it should be master and sovereign; and that is properly the image of God, for by that only the soul knoweth God and loveth Him. And the nether is likened to a woman, for it should be buxom to the overer party of reason, as woman is buxom to man. And that lieth in knowing and ruling of earthly things, for to use them discreetly after need and for to refuse them when it is no need; for to have aye with it an eye upward to the overer part of reason, with dread and with reverence for to follow it.[1]

---

[1] Underhill, *op. cit.*, pp. 272–3. The source is the *locus classicus*—Augustine's *De Trinitate* XII. *The Cloud of Unknowing* (McCann, *op. cit.*, cc.63–6) follows Richard of St Victor, speaking of powers of the soul rather than parts.

INTRODUCTION

Strictly speaking, the sensuality is distinct from the lower part of the reason, as the "moved" is distinct from the "mover". And this movement may be either in the direction of "an unreasonable beast", or upwards in the direction of the higher part of the reason.[1] Julian, however, simplifies, in identifying mover and moved, the lower part of the reason and the sensuality, and speaks merely of inward and outward, reason or substance, or "the true self" and sensuality.

Hence, when Julian says, at the beginning of her third going forth: "God judgeth us upon our kind substance, which is ever kept whole and safe, one in him; and this judgement is of his righteousness. Man judgeth us upon our changeable sensuality which seemeth now one thing, now another, according as it is dominated by the parts, and sheweth outwards", and, "in as much as [this judgement] is hard and heavy, our good Lord Jesus reformeth it by mercy and grace through the power of his blessed passion" (c.45), we are consonant with her terms of reference. She is speaking of "those that shall be saved"; but she is also speaking of and for those like herself, who are reformed in faith yet feel the weight of sin, and the instinctive attraction to sin, in their lower nature;[2] souls who are conscious of their daily semi-deliberate faults and occasional deliberate venial sins, and perhaps of scruples about serious sins committed in the

---

[1] "Est iterum motiva respondens mota, et haec dicitur sensualitas, movens vero est inferior pars rationis. Et haec sensualitas dupliciter potest habere, nam potest accipi in homine secundum id in quo communicat cum brutis, vel secundum ordinem quem nata est habere ad rationales vires." D. Callus, O.P., "The Powers of the Soul: an early unpublished text", *Recherches de Théologie Ancienne et Médiévale*, XIX (1952), p. 158.

[2] These preliminary chapters (45–50) to the shewing of the Parable fit closely with Hilton's exegesis of Romans 7. 23ff., where reason is the "law in my mind", and sensuality the "law in my members". (Underhill, *op. cit.*, pp. 262–3.)

past: this is the material on which the "variable judgement" is exercised—that we are unworthy and unprofitable servants. The self-blame and agitation which attaches to our failing and sinning, this, Julian had thought, was God's judgement and wrath, and his mercy, the forgiveness of his wrath. But all that she saw in God was the fair, sweet judgement, "in which I saw him assign to us no kind of blame". But the Church's judgement seems to belong to the other, "in which methought I needs must acknowledge myself a sinner; and by the same judgement I understood that sinners are sometimes worthy of blame and wrath". The difficulty is not strictly theological—the theologian will readily agree that the countenance of God is never changed upon us, that "he is ever alike in love", the same today, yesterday and for ever. It is a difficulty only in the context of those who earnestly long for God; Julian admits it to be "a low thing and a simple". But for such souls as hers it can have far-reaching effects, as she indicates in her teaching on the doubtful dreads. For if what we *feel* is true, that all "unpeace" is God's judgement, God's wrath, then many good souls might live in a state of chronic despair. "For methought that to a soul whose whole intent and desire is to love, the wrath of God were harder than any other pain" (c.47).

During the time of her sickness, Julian had experienced the alternation of consolation and desolation; there she was taught that "it is expedient to some souls to have experience in this wise—sometimes to be in comfort, and sometimes to lack comfort and to be left to themselves. It is God's will that we know that he keepeth us surely, ever the same in woe and in weal; and that for profit of his soul a man is sometimes left to himself, without his sin always being the cause" (c.15). It is this teaching which she develops in these chapters which lead up to the Parable. The work of the Holy Spirit in the soul is to reconcile the outward with the inward; but often, in the deferment of our hope, the fulfilment of our longing sight, we fall back into our frail blind self; for "this passing life that we lead here, in our sensuality, is not aware of what our true self is, except in faith" (c.46). It is through this feeling that we are left to ourselves, that we "fall into sorrow and tempest" and are "often dead, according to man's judgement on earth". Again, if we take the words out of her context, we could suspect her of a highly unorthodox view. But as it is, we see that she is speaking of that painful darkness and state of abandonment in which the soul, as she strives to read her own conscience (a conscience formed according to the teaching of the Church), is convinced that God has, and rightly, cast her off. Julian has so well understood this state of mind, that even though she sees that "in the sight of God, the soul that shall be safe was never dead nor shall ever be"[1] (c.50), she cannot rest until she is enlightened.

The Parable of the Lord and the Servant (c.51), the "misty" answer to Julian's prayer for further enlightenment, is, by any standards, allegorical writing of the highest quality. At a time when the *exemplum* seems to have outlived its usefulness even as a rhetorical device, Julian is witness that the form is ageless: that it will always appeal, given the true artistic correspondence between the truth and its vesture. Its hallmarks are simplicity, clarity and the relevance of the pictorial detail. It is true medieval allegory—the scriptural analogy is immediately apparent in the suffering servant of the prophet Isaias:

> Behold my servant shall understand, he shall be exalted, and extolled, and shall be exceeding high. . . . Surely he

---

[1] "But the souls of the just are in the hand of God, and the torment of death shall not touch them. In the sight of the unwise they seemed to die . . . but they are at peace." (Wisdom 3.1–3.)

> hath borne our infirmities and carried our sorrows: and we have thought him as it were a leper, and as one struck by God and afflicted. But he was wounded for our iniquities, he was bruised for our sins: the chastisement of our peace was upon him, and by his bruises we are healed. All we like sheep have gone astray, everyone hath turned aside into his own way: and the Lord hath laid on him the iniquity of us all . . . he hath done no iniquity, neither was there deceit in his mouth. And the Lord was pleased to bruise him in infirmity; if he shall lay down his life for sin, he shall see a long-lived seed, and the will of the Lord shall be prosperous in his hand. Because his soul hath laboured, he shall see and be filled: by his knowledge shall this my just servant justify many, and he shall bear their iniquities.[1]

So Julian saw that the servant was shewed for Christ and for Adam; and Adam is every man that shall be saved—the "long-lived seed" of Christ in whom is the Father; the seed brought forth, nurtured by Mercy and Grace in the again-making—but in all Christ, God and Man; who fell, with Adam, into the deeps of the Maiden's womb, our Sensuality taking and reforming (in us) by Mercy and Grace. So that the look of the Lord on his servant is only pity and ruth for his falling and his hard pains: and a blissful looking for his victory ("Father, glorify thy name"). The dynamism of the eternal Wisdom—of the God who "so loved the world that he sent his Son, that men might not perish but might find life through him", is, in a manner, caught and held in the web of Julian's tapestry.

The chapters which spring from the shewing of the parable are an elaboration of the Pauline doctrine of the incorporation into Christ of all that shall be saved. "For in that

---

[1] Isaias 52. 13; 53. 4–7, 10–11.

same time that God knit himself to our body in the Maiden's womb, he took our sensual soul. In taking which, having enclosed us all in himself, he oned it to our substance. For Christ, having knit to himself every man that shall be saved, is perfect man." This is the completed growth of Christ, of which St Paul speaks in the epistle to the Ephesians.[1] And it is the great texts of the epistle to the Colossians which re-echo again and again as we ponder Julian's explanations of *Kind, Substance and Sensuality*:

> In the Son of God, in his blood, we find the redemption which sets us free from our sins. He is the true likeness of the God we cannot see; his is the first birth which precedes every act of creation. Yes, in him all created things took their being, heavenly and earthly, visible and invisible. . . They were created through him and in him; he takes precedency of all, and in him all subsist. He too is that head whose body is the Church; it begins with him, since his was the first birth out of death; thus in every way the primacy was to come his. It was God's good pleasure to let all completeness dwell in him, and through him to win back all things, whether in heaven or on earth, into union with himself, making peace with them through his blood.[2]

It is with this for background that Julian says:

> God is kind in his Being. That is to say, the Goodness which is Kind, is God. He is the Ground: he is the Sub-

---

[1] ". . . so we shall reach perfect manhood, that maturity which is proportioned to the completed growth of Christ . . . and so grow up, in everything, into a due proportion with Christ, who is our head. On him all the body depends; it is organized and unified by each contact with the source which supplies it; and thus, each limb receiving the active power it needs, it achieves its natural growth, building itself up through Charity" (4. 13, 15, 16).

[2] Colossians 1. 14–19. And cf. 2. 9–10.

INTRODUCTION

stance: he is the very thing called Kindness. And he is the very Father and the very Mother of kinds. And all kinds that he hath made to flow out of him to work his will, they must be restored and brought again into him, by the salvation of man, through the working of grace. For of all the kinds that he hath set in various creatures separately, only in man is all the whole—in fullness and in power, in beauty and in goodness, in royalty and nobility... This fair kind, it is general; it is our precious Mother, Christ. For him was this fair kind prepared: for the worship and nobility of man's making and for the joy and the bliss of man's salvation; just as he saw, understood and knew it, from without-beginning (c.62).

In considering Julian's use of the word *kind* and its cognates in this and similar passages, it is necessary to notice that certain distinctions, which are now part of our theological terminology and thinking, were by no means widely current in Julian's time. This is particularly so of the precise distinction which modern theologians draw between "natural" and "supernatural". Hence, though "kind" and "kindly" are exact linguistic equivalents for "nature" and "natural", theologically speaking Julian's use of these terms is much more concrete than ours. Hence when she says "our kindly will is to have God" she is not thinking of the "natural desire for God" in the modern theological sense—having in mind a hypothetical purely natural man whom God might have created in another order of existence, in which man would not have been destined to share the Divine Nature. Similarly, when she says: "... it was in his endless purpose to make man's kind. Which fair kind was first prepared for his own Son, the second Person" (c.58), she is not taking sides in the theological controversy as to whether Christ would have become man if Adam had not sinned. These hypotheses do not enter into Julian's thinking. What she sees is the Divine plan from without-beginning, the Divine order as it was, is and shall be, the Divine working in the concrete. "By the endless purpose and decision and the full accord of the Trinity, the second Person was to be the ground and head of this fair human kind; of him we are all sprung, in him we are all enclosed, to him we shall all go; finding in him our full heaven in everlasting joy; according to the foreseeing purpose of all the Blessed Trinity from without-beginning" (c.53). Hence she is not concerned to distinguish precisely between God's gifts which are due to us because we are men, and the gifts of grace which are given because we are made "partakers of the Divine Nature". For "we are indebted to God for Kind, and we are indebted to God for grace" (c.61); "Kind and grace are one accord. For grace is God, and unmade Kind is God. He is two, in manner of working (but one in love): and neither of them worketh without the other—they may not be parted" (c.63). Among her many references to the working of the Blessed Trinity in man's soul is the trilogy life, love and light, three attributes in God "seen in one goodness; into which goodness my reason would be oned—cleaving to it with all its might. I beheld with reverent dread, highly marvelling in the feeling of the sweet accord—that our reason is in God, understanding that it is the highest gift that we have received; and it is grounded in Kind" (c.83). It would be absurd to think that this is a disparagement of strictly supernatural gifts. By "reason", here, Julian means the "sovereign point of the spirit".[1] She has already described faith as "a power that cometh from our kind substance into our sensual soul, by the Holy Ghost. In which power, all our virtues come to us; for without that, no man may receive virtues" (c.54). "Faith", she says, "cometh from the kind

[1] Cf. infra, p. 37.

INTRODUCTION

love of our soul, and from the clear light of our reason, and from the steadfast mind which we have of God, in our first making" (c.55).[1] Faith is the light of "our endless day that is our Father, God"; it is "the cause of our life". This light is the blessed Trinity; and it is Charity. For "Charity unmade is God, and charity made is our soul in God" (c.83).

In Julian's scheme, then, there is no place for an abstract psychology which is to serve as an introduction to a dogmatic treatise on man's creation and his elevation to the supernatural. When she thinks and speaks of the powers and the parts of the soul, she looks constantly at the Trinity working in the "making and the again-making". Reason is indeed the higher part of the soul, as the sensuality is the lower part—those powers of man's kind which depend on the body in their operation. But "our kind is in God, wholly ... our kind, which is the higher part, is knit to God in the making; and God is knit to our kind which is the lower part, in taking of our flesh. And thus in Christ our two kinds are oned; for Christ is comprehended in the Trinity, in whom our higher part is grounded and rooted; and our lower part the second Person hath taken—which kind was first prepared for him" (c.57). By "reason", Julian does not understand merely the intellectual power, but also that "loving power", of which the author of the *Cloud* speaks so lucidly.[2]

[1] This is the traditional classification of the "principal powers of the soul" (cf. the *Cloud*, McCann, *op. cit.*, p. 85), mind, understanding and will, the "made trinity".

[2] "But since all reasonable creatures, angel and man, have in them ... one principal working power, the which is called a knowing power, and another principal working power, the which is called a loving power. Of the which two powers, to the first, the which is a knowing power, God who is the maker of them is evermore incomprehensible; but to the second, the which is the loving power, he is, in every man diversely, all comprehensible to the full. In so much, that one loving soul alone in itself, by virtue of love, may comprehend in itself him. . ." McCann, *op. cit.*, pp. 9–10.

INTRODUCTION

"For ere that he made us, he loved us; and when we were made we loved him. This is a love made of the divine substantial Love of the Holy Ghost,[1] mighty by reason of the Power of the Father, wise in the consciousness of the Wisdom of the Son. Thus is man's soul made by God, and in the same moment knit to God... In this endless love man's soul[2] is kept whole, as all the matter of the Revelations meaneth and sheweth; in which endless love we are led and preserved by God, and never shall be lost" (c. 53).

Here then is the full context of the godly will. "This will is so good that it may never will evil, but evermore, continually, it willeth good and worketh good in the sight of God. Our Lord willeth that we know this in faith and belief; and especially, that we have all this blessed will whole and safe in our Lord Jesus Christ. For this same kind, with which heaven shall be filled,[3] must needs be according to God's righteousness, so knit and oned in him, that in it must be preserved a substance which never could nor should be separated from him" (c. 53). It cannot be coincidental that one of the great topics of thirteenth-century theological discussion was the *synderesis* and its *scintilla*: *synderesis* being the higher part of the soul, and the *scintilla* its supreme point.[4] For many of Julian's predecessors and contemporaries, this "sovereign point of the spirit" is the seat of the

---

[1] "The love of God has been poured out in our hearts by the Holy Spirit, whom we have received" (Romans 5. 5).

[2] We must remind ourselves constantly that Julian is speaking only of them that shall be saved.

[3] Heaven is to be filled with the kind of angels, as well as of men.

[4] This is, of course, to simplify. There were two approaches to the problem, moral and affective. Today, the word lives on in scholastic theology only in its moral aspect. Again, some theologians identified the two terms. So St Thomas Aquinas speaks of the *synderesis* as the *scintilla conscientae*, which flies above the conscience like the spark above the fire, and attains a direct (intuitional) contact with the Divine truth.

mystical faculty—the "place" where "is made the marriage betwixt God and the soul".[1] One of them defines it thus: "The supreme point of the loving power, chief and uncontaminated participation in that Divine Goodness which flows from the Truth into its image, ineffably distinct from all that is beneath it, which passes as it were into the Divine Life, and, in a manner which defies description, is deified."[2] The language is, indeed, quite foreign to Julian's way of speaking; but there is a clear similarity of thought: "A high understanding it is, inwardly, to see and to know that God, who is our Maker, dwelleth in our soul. And a higher understanding it is, and more inwardly, to see and to know that our soul, that is made, dwelleth in God in substance. Of which substance, by God, we are what we are. And I saw no difference between God and our substance; but as it were all God. And yet my understanding took it that our substance is in God; that is to say, that God is God and our substance is a creature in God."[3]

Whether or not Julian was aware of a common opinion of thirteenth-century theologians, that the *scintilla* is never extinguished, not even by mortal sin,[4] is not really of consequence. For though the doctrine of the *synderesis* and its *scintilla* throws considerable light on Julian's teaching concerning the incorporation into Christ, in that it elucidates her meaning of the words *kind*, *substance*, *reason* and *sensuality* in their fourteenth-century context, yet it would be a mistake to suppose that the *scintilla* is to be identified with Julian's godly will. More than once she emphasizes that she

[1] Hodgson, *op. cit.*, p. 56.

[2] The words of Thomas Gallus, in a commentary on the Canticle of Canticles. Gallus is the "Abbot of St Victor" of the author of the *Cloud*.

[3] C. 54. We recall that with Julian "substance" is a synonym for reason, the higher part of the soul.

[4] Cf. O. Lottin, O.S.B., *Psychologie et Morale au XXIe et XIIIe siècles* (Louvain, 1948), t.II, 1e partie, pp. 103ff.

was never shewn any one soul "in special" except that of our blessed Lady. She did not even see that she herself belonged to the number of the predestined, except "in hope". Her intellectual vision of the penitent-saints was also a shewing "in general"—of a procession of saints "without number" (c.38). The godly will is that "blessed will" which is kept whole and safe in our Lord Jesus Christ: it is in man's *kind*, i.e. all those that shall be saved, in general and not in special, which "is so knit and oned to him, that in it must be preserved a substance which never could nor should be separated from him" (c.53). She has nothing to say of the precise way in which the individual predestined soul, in this life, participates in this blessed will. She never even raises, let alone answers, the question "How can a man sin, and yet not lose charity?"

Dom Roger Hudleston,[1] in his comments on Julian's first reference to the godly will, opines that her teaching here is unorthodox, but excuses her on the ground that William of St Thierry, whose works in Julian's time were ascribed to St Bernard, taught that David and St Peter, when they sinned, did not lose charity.[2] William's context is that of St John's first Epistle: "Whosoever is born of God, committeth not sin: for his seed abideth in him, and he cannot sin,

[1] *The Revelations of Divine Love* (London, 1952), pp. xxiii ff., 174–5.

[2] "Abbot William belongs to the twelfth century and his teaching on this point may be regarded as one of those pre-scholastic opinions which were inevitably dismissed when the great scholastics worked out their scientific theology. But Abbot William's writings remained in circulation and since they were very commonly ascribed to St Bernard obtained all the authority of that great name." Since Fr Hudleston wrote these words, the Abbot William has been re-habilitated in no uncertain fashion. Cf. Bouyer, *The Cistercian Heritage* (London, 1958). Fr Hudleston's reference is to William's *De Natura et Dignitate Amoris*, c.vi (Migne, *Patres Latini*, CLXXXIV, 389–90). St Thomas does not dispose of William's proposition, as Fr Hudleston alleges, but explains it *secundum mentem auctoris*, as the editor of Migne demonstrates (*loc. cit.*).

INTRODUCTION

because he is born of God."[1] Speaking of David, William says, "When he sinned he did not lose charity, but charity was somehow stunned in him". "A rhetorical way of speaking", says William's editor: "just as he explains 'he who is born of God cannot sin' as 'may not persevere in sin'." Another twelfth-century theologian, Hugh of St Victor, also concerns himself with the same words of St John *vis-à-vis* the sins of David and St Peter, and the difference between the predestined and the reproved, in respect of mortal sin. Hugh sums up as follows: "None of the predestined end this life in an evil state, since those that shall be saved are so ordained and given to Christ 'that they might not perish but have eternal life'. Of these St John says: 'we know that everyone born of God sins not'. David sinned grievously, but because he was born of God and belonged to the society of the sons of God, he did not sin finally (*non peccavit usque ad mortem*), but through his penitence merited pardon. Of this final sin, John makes mention in these words: 'There is a sin unto death' (1 Joan. v). And he immediately adds: 'Whosoever is born of God sinneth not.'"[2]

We may say, if we will, that Julian approximates to this view, that in her treatment of the godly will, she is speaking of the "many other ways in which the Spirit of God can remain with a man, even when he has left him in respect of the gift of Charity".[3] But even when she says: "But now I needs must tell you in what manner I saw deadly sin in those creatures who would not die because of sin, but would live without end in the joy of God", she has no intention of discussing how it is possible for one of the predestined to be separated from this blessed will of Christ temporarily, or what his precise theological position might be during that time. She is, as usual, concerned with those whose whole

---

[1] 3. 9. [2] *De Sacramentis*, II, XII. Migne, PL CLXXVI, 550.
[3] Hugh of St Victor, *ibid.* 547.

intent is set on loving God; who feel as Peter felt when he cried, at Christ's feet: "Depart from me, for I am a sinful man." So she explains: "As long as we have anything to do with sin, we shall never see clearly this blissful look of God. And the more horrible and grievous our sins are, the deeper are we, for that time, out of this blessed sight. And therefore it seemeth to us, oftentimes, as though we were in peril of death and in a part of hell; because of the sorrow and pain that sin meaneth to us. And thus we are dead for the time—out of very sight of our blissful life" (c.72). In her teaching on the Motherhood of Christ—the logical development of her anthropology—she re-emphasizes the same points: "When we are strengthened by his sweet working, then we deliberately choose him, by his grace, to be his servants and his lovers, lastingly without end. And yet, after this, he suffereth some of us to fall more hard and more grievously than ever we did before—or so it would seem. . . He willeth that we betake us mightily to the faith of Holy Church. . . For a single person may often be broken —or so it seemeth to the self. But the whole Body of the Church was never broken, nor ever shall be, without end. And therefore a sure thing it is, a good and a gracious, to will, meekly and mightily, to be fastened and oned to our Mother Holy Church: that is, Christ Jesus" (c.61).

The whole purpose of Julian's writing is that her even-Christians may be sped in the way of salvation. Her "comfortable words" to them develop the text of St Paul: "He whose power is at work in us is powerful enough, and more than powerful enough, to carry out his purpose beyond all our hopes and dreams."[1] For he "strengtheneth the creature above the self". "And thus I understood that what man or woman deliberately chooseth God in this life, for love, may be sure that he is loved without end. Which endless love

[1] Ephesians 3. 20.

INTRODUCTION

worketh in him that grace. For he willeth us to hold trustfully to this—that we be as sure, in hope, of the bliss of heaven whilst we are here, as we shall be, in certainty, when we are there" (c.65).

The sixteenth revelation—the fourth and final entry into the cavern of God's wisdom—is granted to strengthen this hope (cc.68–86). The blindness and darkness, which are the effects of the first sin and all the sins following it that are of our contriving, become profitable to us in faith and hope. They belong to the fire of tribulation in which our fair kind is tried, and found to be without defect (c.63). Though this night is the cause of all our pain and woe, yet in it, faith, which is "a light coming from our endless day, that is, our Father, God," shines in the darkness (c.83). And though it is only by his light, the mercy of his grace, that we can see that we are what we are, "and how horrible our sin is"; yet the sight of the Indwelling shows how tenderly and preciously we are loved, and assures us that the darkness, pain and woe are profitable. "Marvellous and stately is the place where the Lord dwelleth. And therefore he willeth that we readily turn us to his gracious touching, having more joy in his all-love than sorrow in our frequent fallings. For of anything that we may do, it is most worship to him that we live, in our penance, gladly and merrily for his love. For he beholdeth us so tenderly that he seeth all our living here to be a penance. For the kind longing in us for him is a lasting penance in us. Which penance he worketh in us, and mercifully helpeth us to bear it" (c.81).

"Fear not, little flock, for it hath pleased your Father to give you a kingdom."[1] Julian addresses herself to the little and simple souls of Christ, rather than to those that be very wise. We may believe that our Lord would have them know a little more, through her, of these high doctrines which are

[1] Luke 12. 38.

the wisdom and knowledge of the Church's treasure—his dwelling in us, and our incorporation into him. It is not the wise and the learned who are inwardly affected by the sinfulness of the world about them, but the little and simple who seem to see the reflection therein of their own sinful selves. Their very humility makes them doubtful of the fullness of God's love in their own regard. This is the ghostly blindness which most hinders these little and simple—"those men and women who, for God's love, hate sin, and dispose themselves to do God's will" (c.73). This is the doubtful dread, the lack of true trust which enmeshes so many in a mediocrity, in a pusillanimity which effectively bars the way to growth in living faith. Such souls are full of a wrong sort of fear, fear that too much might be asked of them, fear of having to surrender the little material comforts to which they cling so pathetically; or "a dread that is a hindrance to us, through the beholding of ourselves and our sins committed in the past. Because of our sins of every day, because we (or some of us) hold not to our promise, nor keep to the cleanness that our Lord setteth us in, but fall oftentimes into so much wretchedness that it is shame to us to mention it—the beholding of this maketh us so sorrowful and so heavy that we can scarcely see any comfort." The cause of all this, says, Julian, is the unknowing of love. "For some of us believe that God is mighty and may do all; and that he is all-wisdom and can do all; but that he is all-love, and will do all—there we fail." The purpose of the *Revelations* is, simply, to demonstrate that he is all-love, and will do all, to those who are chosen to be the poor in spirit, the meek, the mourners, the clean of heart. His own most "comfortable words" are those recorded in St Matthew's Gospel:

> I confess to thee, O Father, Lord of heaven and earth, because thou hast hid these things from the wise and

INTRODUCTION

prudent, and hast revealed them to little ones. Yea, Father, for so hath it seemed good in thy sight. All things are delivered to me by my Father. And no one knoweth the Son but the Father; neither doth anyone know the Father but the Son, and he to whom it shall please the Son to reveal him. Come to me, all you that labour and are burdened, and I will refresh you. Take my yoke upon you and learn of me, because I am meek and humble of heart: and you shall find rest for your souls. For my yoke is sweet and my burden light.

These verses, in their entirety, may be said to be the full context of the *Revelations of Divine Love*.

REVELATIONS OF DIVINE LOVE

THIS IS A REVELATION OF LOVE THAT JESUS CHRIST, OUR ENDLESS BLISS, MADE IN SIXTEEN SHEWINGS

★

THE FIRST CHAPTER

Of the number of the Revelations, in detail

THE first is of his precious crowning of thorns; and therein was contained and made manifest the Blessed Trinity with the Incarnation and the unity between God and man's soul, with many fair shewings and teachings of endless wisdom and love; in which the shewings that follow are grounded and oned.

The second is of the discolouring of his fair face, which betokened his most dear passion.

The third is that God our Lord all-mighty, all wisdom, all love, as truly as he hath made all things that are, even thus he doeth and worketh all things that are done.

The fourth is the scourging of his tender body, with the plenteous shedding of his precious blood.

The fifth is that the fiend is overcome by the precious passion of Christ.

The sixth is the worshipful thanking of our Lord God, by which he rewardeth all his blessed servants in heaven.

The seventh is our oftentimes experiencing weal and

woe; the experience of weal is a gracious touching and enlightening, with true sureness of endless joy: the experience of woe cometh from temptation, in heaviness and weariness of our mortal life, with a ghostly understanding that we are kept as truly in woe as in weal by the goodness of God.

The eighth is the last pains of Christ, and his cruel dying.

The ninth is of the liking which is in the Blessed Trinity for the hard passion of Christ and his pitiful dying. In which joy and liking he willeth that we be in solace and mirth with him, until we come to the glory in heaven.

The tenth is, our Lord Jesus sheweth, in love, his blessed heart cloven in two.

The eleventh is a high ghostly shewing of his most dear Mother.

The twelfth is that our Lord is all-sovereign being.

The thirteenth is, that our Lord God willeth that we pay great regard to all the deeds which he hath done: to the great nobility of making all things: and to the excellence of man's making, which is above all his works: and to the precious amends he hath made for man's sin, turning all our blame into endless worship. He meaneth thus: "Behold and see! By the same might, wisdom and goodness that I have done all this, by this same might, wisdom and goodness I shall make all well that is not well; and thou shalt see it." And in this he willeth that we keep us in the faith and truth of Holy Church, not wishing to know his secrets, except in so far as this belongeth to us, in this life.

The fourteenth is that our Lord is the ground of our beseeching. Herein were seen two fair properties: one is rightful prayer: the other is true trust: both of which he willeth should be alike large. It is thus that our prayer pleaseth him, and that he with his goodness filleth it full.

The fifteenth is that we shall be taken suddenly from all

our pain and from all our woe; and by his goodness we shall come up above, where we shall have our Lord Jesus for our meed, and be filled full of joy and bliss in heaven.

The sixteenth is that the Blessed Trinity our Maker, in Christ Jesus our Saviour, endlessly dwelleth in our soul, worshipfully ruling and governing all things, us mightily and wisely saving and keeping, for love. And we shall not be overcome by our enemy.

THE SECOND CHAPTER

Of the time of these Revelations; and how she asked three petitions

THESE revelations were shewed to a simple unlearned creature living in this mortal flesh, in the year of our Lord one thousand three hundred and seventy-three, on the thirteenth day of May.

Before this, the creature desired three gifts of God's grace. The first was mind of the Passion; the second was bodily sickness; the third was to have of God's gift, three wounds. As for the first, I believed that I had experience, to some degree, of the passion of Christ; but I desired to have still more, by the grace of God. I would I had been, that time, with Magdalen and with the others that were Christ's lovers, that I might have seen, bodily, the passion that our Lord suffered for me—that I might have suffered with him as did those others that loved him. And therefore I desired a bodily sight, that I might have more knowledge of the bodily pains of our Saviour, and of the compassion of our Lady and of all his true lovers that were living at that time and saw his pains. I would I had been one of them and had suffered with them. Other sight or shewing of God desired I never none until the soul should be separated from the body—(I believed I would be saved, by God's mercy). And this was my intention—that I should afterwards, because of that shewing, have more true mind of the passion of Christ.

As for the second gift, there came to my mind, without any seeking, an earnest desire to have of God's gift a bodily sickness. I desired this sickness to be grievous even unto death (as long as, in that sickness, I might receive all the rites of Holy Church); I myself believing that I was going to die, and all creatures that saw me supposing the same. I wanted no manner of comfort either of the flesh or worldly life in that sickness; but I desired to have all the pains, bodily and ghostly, that I should have if I were about to die—all the dreads, temptations of fiends, and all manner of pains except the departing of the soul. Such was my meaning; for I desired, by the mercy of God, to be purified; so as afterwards to live more according to the worship of God because of that sickness. I hoped that this would stand to my credit when I should come to die (for I desired to be with my God and Maker soon).

These two desires, of the passion and of the sickness, I desired of him with a condition; for I believed that mine was not the ordinary use of prayer. Therefore I said: "Lord, thou knowest what I will—but only if it be thy will that I have it. If it be not thy will, good Lord, be not displeased; for I will only as thou wilt." This sickness I desired in my youth—to have it when I was thirty years old.

As for the third gift, by the grace of God and the teaching of Holy Church, I conceived a mighty desire to receive three wounds in my life; that is to say, the wound of true contrition, the wound of kind compassion, and the wound of earnest longing for God. And just as I asked for the other two with a condition, so I asked for the third mightily and without any condition. The two desires aforesaid passed from my mind; but the third dwelt there continually.

THE THIRD CHAPTER

Of the sickness obtained of God by petition

AND when I was thirty years and a half, God sent me a bodily sickness; in which I lay three days and three nights. And on the fourth night I received all the rites of Holy Church, and thought not to have lived till day. And after this I lay two days and two nights more. And on the third night, I thought oftentimes that I would pass away; and so thought they that were with me. And yet in this time I felt a great loathsomeness to die—not for anything on earth that I wished to live for, nor for any pain that I was afraid of (for I trusted in God and his mercy), but for this: I wished to live in order to love God better and for a longer time, that I might, by the grace of that living, have more knowing and loving of God in the bliss of heaven. (For I considered all the time that I had lived here to be so little and short in the sight of that endless bliss.) Then I thought: "Good Lord, perhaps my living any longer may not be to thy worship?" And I understood in my reason, and by the pains I felt, that I was going to die. And I assented fully with all the will of my heart to be at God's disposal.

Thus I endured until day; and by then my body, as regards feeling, was dead from the middle downwards. Then I was helped up into a sitting position—and propped up, to give a greater freedom to my heart: that I might be at God's disposal, thinking on him while my life should last. My curate was sent for to be present at my end. Before he came, my eyes were fixed upwards, and I could not speak. He set the cross before my face, and said: "I have brought the image of thy Saviour; look thereupon, and comfort thee therewith." But I believed I was well enough; for my eyes were set upwards into heaven whither I trusted to come by the mercy of God. Nevertheless, I consented to turn my eyes to confront the crucifix, if I could. And so I did. For I believed that I could endure longer looking straight forward than upwards. After this, my sight began to fail; and the chamber around me grew as dark as if it had been night, except about the image of the cross where the daylight remained (I knew not how). All the place by the cross was ugly and fearful to me, as though it were occupied by many fiends.

After this, the upper part of my body began to die—so much so that I had scarcely any feeling at all. My greatest pain was shortness of breath and the failing of life. And I thought truly that I would die. But then, suddenly, all my pain was taken from me and I was as right, especially in the upper part of my body, as ever I was before. I marvelled at this sudden change—it seemed to be a secret working of God, and not of kind. And yet I did not any the more believe that I should live because of feeling easier; and the feeling of this ease was no full ease to me. "No", I thought, "I would rather be freed from this world"—my heart was earnestly set thereupon.

Then it came suddenly to my mind that I should desire the second wound, that of our Lord's gift and of his grace I might be filled full, in body and in mind, with experience of his blessed passion, as I had prayed before. For I would that his pains were my pains, with compassion, and afterwards with longing unto God. Thus, I believed, I might with his grace obtain the wounds that I had desired before. But in all this I desired never any bodily sight, nor any manner of shewing of God: but only compassion— such as I believed a kindred soul might have with our Lord Jesus, who, for love, willed to become a mortal man. With him I desired to suffer whilst I lived in this mortal body, according as God would give me the grace.

THE FOURTH CHAPTER

Here beginneth the first Revelation, of the precious crowning of Christ, etc., as described in the first chapter; and how God filleth the heart full of the utmost joy; and of his great meekness; and how the sight of the passion of Christ is sufficient strength against every temptation of the fiends; and of the great excellence and meekness of the blessed Virgin Mary

AND in this time, suddenly I saw the red blood running down from under the garland, hot and fresh, plenteous and life-like, just as it was in the time that the garland of thorns was pressed down on his blessed head. Even so I conceived truly that it was himself, God and man, the same that suffered for me, who shewed it to me—without any intermediary.

In the same shewing, suddenly the Trinity filled full my heart with the utmost joy (thus I understood it shall be in heaven without end unto all that come thither). For the Trinity is God, and God is the Trinity. The Trinity is our Maker. The Trinity is our Keeper. The Trinity is our everlasting Lover. The Trinity is our endless Joy and our Bliss, by our Lord Jesus Christ and in our Lord Jesus Christ. And this was shewed in the first sight and in them all. For where Jesus appeareth, the Blessed Trinity is understood, as I see it.

And I said: "Lord, bless us!" This I said with reverence for my meaning, in a mighty voice. For I was truly astounded by the wonder and the marvel, that he who is so reverend and dreadful should be so homely with a sinful creature still living in this wretched flesh. I took it that in this time our Lord Jesus, of his courteous love, wished to shew me comfort before the time of my temptation. For (I thought) it might well be that, by the permission of God and with his keeping, I should be tempted by fiends before I died. With this sight of his blessed passion, and with the Godhead that I saw in my understanding, I knew well that there was strength enough for me (and indeed for all living creatures that shall be saved) against all the fiends of hell, and against all ghostly enemies.

In this time he brought our Lady, Saint Mary, to my understanding. I saw her ghostly, in bodily likeness; a simple maiden and a meek: young of age, little more than a child—in the same stature as she was when she conceived. God also shewed me, in part, the wisdom and the truth of her soul. Wherein I understood the reverent beholding with which she beheld her God, who is her Maker; she marvelled, with great reverence, that he willed to be born of her that was a simple creature of his making. For this was her marvelling—that he who was her Maker, willed to be born of her who was made. And this wisdom and truth—this knowing of the greatness of her Maker, and the littleness of herself that is made, made her to say full meekly to Gabriel, "Lo me here, God's handmaiden!" In this sight I understood truly that she is more in worthiness and in fullness of grace than all that God made beneath her. For nothing that is made is above her except the blessed manhood of Christ, as I see it.

THE FIFTH CHAPTER

How God is to us everything that is good, tenderly wrapping us round; and everything that is made is nothing in regard to Almighty God; and how man hath no rest until he counteth himself and all things as nothing, for the love of God

IN the same time that I saw this sight of his head bleeding, our good Lord shewed a ghostly sight of his homely loving. I saw that he is to us everything that is good and strengthening for our help. He is our clothing that, for love, wrappeth us up and windeth us about; embraceth us, all becloseth us and hangeth about us, for tender love; so that he can never leave us. And so, in this sight, I saw that he is to us everything that is good, as I understand it.

Also in this he shewed a little thing, the size of a hazelnut, which seemed to lie in the palm of my hand; and it was as round as any ball. I looked upon it with the eye of my understanding, and thought, "What may this be?" I was answered in a general way, thus: "It is all that is made." I wondered how long it could last; for it seemed as though it might suddenly fade away to nothing, it was so small. And I was answered in my understanding: "It lasts, and ever shall last; for God loveth it. And even so hath everything being— by the love of God."

In this little thing I saw three properties. The first is that God made it: the second, that God loveth it: the third, that God keepeth it. And what beheld I in this? Truly, the Maker, the Lover and the Keeper. And until I am substantially oned to him, I can never have full rest nor true bliss; that is to say, until I am so fastened to him that there is no created thing at all between my God and me. And this little thing that is made—it seemed as though it would fade away to nothing, it was so small. We need to have knowledge of this—that we should reckon as naught everything that is made, to love and have God who is unmade. For this is the reason why we are not all in ease of heart and of soul: that we seek here rest in this thing that is so little and where no rest is in; we know not our God that is almighty, all-wise and all-good. For he is very rest. It is his will to be known and it is his pleasure that we rest us in him. All that is beneath him sufficeth not to us. And this is the reason why no soul can be in rest until it is naughted of everything that is made. When the soul is willingly naughted, for love, so as to have him who is All, then is she able to receive ghostly rest.

And also our good Lord shewed that it is the greatest pleasure to him that a simple soul come to him nakedly, plainly and homely. This is the kind yearning of the soul, through the touching of the Holy Ghost, as I am given to understand by this shewing:

> God, of thy goodness, give me thyself; for thou art enough to me, and I can nothing ask that is less that would be full worship of thee. And if I ask anything that is less, ever me wanteth; for in thee only have I all.

These words, through the goodness of God, are full lovesome to the soul, and full near touch the will of our Lord. For his goodness full filleth all his creatures and all his blessed works, without end. For he is the endlessness, and he made us only for himself; and he restored us by his blessed passion, and ever keepeth us in his blessed love. And all this is of his goodness.

THE SIXTH CHAPTER

How we should pray; of the great tender love that our Lord hath to man's soul—wishing us to be occupied in the knowing and loving of him

THIS shewing was given, as I understand it, to teach our soul wisely to cleave to the goodness of God. And in that same time our customary manner of praying was brought to my mind—how, because of unknowing of love, we employ many means. Then I saw truly that it is greater worship to God, and truly more delightful to him, if we pray to himself and of his goodness, and cleave thereunto, by his grace, with true understanding and steadfast belief, than if we used all the means that heart can think. For to use all these is too little, and not full worship to God. For in his goodness is all the whole, and therein faileth nothing at all.

There came into my mind at this same time these things, as I shall say. We pray to God by his holy flesh, by his precious blood, his holy passion, his most dear death and worshipful wounds. But all the blessed kindness and the endless life that we have because of all this—it is of the goodness of God. And we pray him by the sweet love of the Mother that bore him; but all the help that we have because of her—it is of his goodness. And we pray by his holy cross on which he died; but all the help and all the power that we have because of that cross—it is of his goodness. And in the same wise, all the help that we have of special saints, and of all the blessed company of heaven, the very dear love and holy endless friendship that we have of them—it is of his goodness. The means that the goodness of God hath ordained to help us are full fair and many; of which the chief and most eminent means is the blessed kind which he took of the Maiden, along with all the means, belonging to our redemption and to our endless salvation, which went before and come after.

Wherefore it pleaseth him that we seek him and worship him by these means: but understanding and knowing that he is the goodness of them all. For the highest prayer is to the goodness of God which cometh down to us, to the lowest part of our need. It quickeneth our soul, and maketh it to live; it maketh it to grow in grace and in virtue; it is nearest it in kind, and readiest to it in grace; it is, indeed, the very grace for which the soul seeketh and ever shall, until we know our God truly—he that hath us all beclosed in himself.

Man goeth upright; his food is taken and hidden in his body as in a very fine purse. And in the time of his necessity the purse is opened, and then it is shut again—all in seemly fashion. That it is God that worketh this, is shewed there where it is said: "He cometh down to us, to the lowest part of our need". For he despiseth nothing of what he hath made. And he disdaineth not to serve us in the simplest offices that belong, in kind, to our body, for love of the soul that is made to his own likeness. For as the body is clad in clothes, and the flesh in skin, and the bones in flesh, and the heart in the breast; so are we, soul and body, clad and enclosed in the goodness of God. Yea, and more homely; for they all vanish, wasting away. But the goodness of God is ever whole and most near to us, without any comparison. Truly our Lover desireth that the soul cleave to him with all its might; so that we are clinging, ever more and more, to his goodness. For of all things that heart can conceive, this most pleaseth God and soonest bringeth profit. Our soul is so preciously loved by him that is highest that it passeth beyond the knowing of all creatures. That is to say, there is no creature made that can know how much and how sweetly and how tenderly our Maker loveth us. Therefore we may, with his grace and his help, stand in ghostly beholding with everlasting marvelling in this high, overpassing, immeasurable love that our Lord hath towards us, of his goodness.

And therefore we may ask of our Lover all that we will; for our kindly will is to have God, and the good will of God is to have us. Nor may we ever cease willing or loving, until we have him in fullness of joy. And then we may no more will. It is his will that we be occupied in knowing and loving until the time come that we be full filled in heaven; therefore was this lesson of love shewed, as ye shall see. For the strength and ground of all was shewed in the first sight. For above all things, the beholding and the loving of the Maker maketh the soul to seem least in its own sight, and most filleth it with reverent dread and true meekness, and with plenty of charity towards its even-christians.

THE SEVENTH CHAPTER

How our Lady, beholding the greatness of her Maker, thought herself the least; and of the great drops of blood running from under the garland; and how man's greatest joy is that the most high and mighty God is the holiest and most courteous

AND to teach us thus, as I understand it, our good Lord shewed our Lady Saint Mary in that same time; that is, the high wisdom and truth that she had in the beholding of her Maker. This wisdom and truth made her to behold her God as so great, so high, so mighty and so good that the greatness and nobleness of this beholding her God filled her full of reverent dread. And with this, she saw herself as so little and so low, so simple and so poor in regard of her God, that this reverent dread filled her full of meekness. Thus—in this ground—she was filled full of grace and of all manner of virtues, and surpasseth all creatures.

And in all the time that he shewed this, that I have just told you, in ghostly sight, I saw continually the bodily sight of the head bleeding freely. The great drops of blood fell down from under the garland like pellets; they seemed to come straight out of the veins. As they came out they were a reddish brown, and the blood was very thick; but in their spreading forth they were bright red. And when they came to the eye-brows, there they vanished.

And though the bleeding continued until many things were seen and understood, nevertheless, the beauty and the life-like quality were there continually. And the plentifulness of the blood was like to the drops of water that fall from the eaves of a house after a great shower of rain—when they fall so thick that no man, by his ordinary senses, can count them. In their roundness as they spread over the forehead, they were like to the scale of the herring. These three comparisons came into my mind at the time: pellets, for the roundness of the drops, as they came forth: the scale of the herring, for their roundness as they spread: rain-drops from the eaves of a house, for the plentifulness innumerable.

This shewing was vivid and life-like, hideous and dreadful, sweet and lovely. But of all the sights that I saw, this was the greatest comfort to me: that our good Lord who is so reverend and dreadful is also so homely and so courteous. And this most filled me full of liking, and sureness of soul.

For the understanding of this, he shewed me this simple example. The greatest worship that a mighty being or a great lord can do to a poor servant, if he wills to be homely with him, is to shew himself, as he truly is, both in private and publicly, with a glad countenance. Then thinketh the poor creature thus: "Lo! What more could this noble lord do, that is more worship and joy to me, than to shew this marvellous homeliness to me who am so little? In truth, this is greater joy and liking to me than if he gave me great gifts and remained himself a stranger to me."

This example, though it was shewed bodily, was so profound that a man's heart might be so carried away that he could almost forget himself in the joy of this great homeliness. And so it cometh to pass in respect of our Lord Jesus and ourselves. For truly, it is the greatest joy that could be, as I see it, that he who is highest and mightiest, noblest and worthiest, is the lowest and meekest, homeliest and most courteous. In deed and in truth, this marvellous joy shall he shew to us all, when we see him. And this is our Lord's will, that we have belief and trust, joy and liking, comfort and great solace in so far as we may, with his grace and with his help, unto the time that we see it truly. For the perfect fullness of joy that we shall have, as I see it, is this marvellous courtesy and homeliness from our Father, who is our Maker in our Lord Jesus Christ—who is our Brother and our Saviour.

Yet no man, in this life, can know this marvellous homeliness, except he have it by special shewing of our Lord, or by great plenty of grace, inwardly given by the Holy Ghost. But faith and belief, with charity, deserve this gift; and so it is received by grace. For in faith, together with hope and charity, our life is grounded. And the shewing, which is made to whomsoever God willeth, plainly teacheth the same, but openly, and setting forth many secret things that belong to our faith and belief, which it is worshipful to know. When the shewing, which is given for a time, is passed and vanished, then faith keepeth it, by the grace of the Holy Ghost, until our life's end.

Thus, in the shewing is seen none other than the faith, neither less nor more, as may be seen by our Lord's meaning in the same matter.

THE EIGHTH CHAPTER

A recapitulation of what is said; and how this was shewed to her for all in general

As long as I saw this sight of the plenteous bleeding of the head, I could not stint of these words—"Lord, bless us". And in this shewing I understood six things: the first is the tokens of his blessed passion; the second is the Maiden that is his most dear Mother; the third is the blessed Godhead that ever was and is and shall be—all-might, all-wisdom and all-love; the fourth is everything that he hath made—for well I know that heaven and earth and all that is made is great and large and fair and good; but the reason why it shewed so little to my sight was that I saw it in the presence of him that is the Maker. For to a soul that seeth the Maker of all things, all that is made seemeth full little; the fifth is that he that made all that is made, made it for love—and by the same love it is kept, and shall be, without end, as it is before said; the sixth is that God is all that is good, as I see it—and the goodness that all things have, it is he.

All this our Lord shewed in the first sight, and gave me space and time to behold it. Then the bodily sight stinted; but the ghostly sight lived on in my understanding. And I abode with reverent dread, rejoicing in what I saw, and desiring, as much as I durst, to see more if it were his will, or the same sight for longer time. In all this I was much affected in charity towards my even-christians—that they might all see and know the same that I saw; for I would that it were a comfort to them. For all this sight was shewed to all, in general.

Then said I to them that were with me: "This day is doomsday for me". This I said because I thought I would die; for on that day that a man or woman dieth, he is judged, particularly: and so he shall be, without end, as I see it. This I said; for I desired them to love God the better, and to make them have mind that this life is short and to see an example of it. In all this time, I thought I would die; and that was, in a way, wonder and marvel to me; because, it seemed, this vision was shewed for them that should live.

All that I say of myself, this I mean to say of the person of all my even-christians. For I am taught in the shewing of our Lord God that such is his meaning. And therefore I pray you all, for God's sake, and counsel you for your own profit, that you cease to notice the wretch that it was shewed to, and mightily, wisely and meekly behold into God; who, of his courteous love and endless goodness willed to shew it generally, unto the comfort of us all. For it is God's will that you receive it with as great a joy and liking as though Jesus had shewed it to you.

THE NINTH CHAPTER

Of the meekness of this woman, keeping herself always in the faith of the Holy Church; and how he that loveth his even-christian for God, loveth all things

I AM not good because of the shewing, but only if I love God the better. And in as much as you love God the better, it is more profit to you than to me. (I say this, not to them that are wise, for they know it well, but to you that are simple, for your ease and comfort; for we are all one in love.) For truly it was not shewed to me that God loveth me better than the least soul that is in grace. And I am sure that there are many that never have shewing nor sight except of the common teaching of Holy Church, who love God better than I. For if I look at myself, as a single person, I am right naught. But if I look to the whole—then I am, in hope, in onehead of charity with all my even-christians. For in this onehead standeth the life of all mankind that shall be saved.

God is all that is good, as I see it. And God hath made all that is made; and God loveth all that he hath made. Thus he that loveth the whole—all his even-christians—for God, loveth all that is. (For in mankind that shall be saved is comprehended all, that is to say, all that is made, and the Maker of all. For in man is God, and in God is all.) He that loveth thus, loveth all. I am hopeful by the grace of God that he who beholdeth it thus shall be truly taught and mightily comforted when he needeth comfort. (I speak of them that shall be saved. For in this time God shewed me no other.)

Yet in all things I believe as Holy Church preacheth and teacheth. For the faith of Holy Church, of which I had understanding beforehand and which, I hope by the grace of God, I will fully keep in use and in custom, stood continually in my sight. It was my will and meaning never to accept anything that could be contrary thereto. With this intent and with this meaning I beheld the shewing with all my diligence. For in all this blessed shewing I beheld it [*sc.* the sight and the faith] as one in God's meaning.

The whole sight was shewed in three parts: by bodily sight, by words formed in my understanding, and by ghostly sight. But the ghostly sight I cannot or may not shew it as clearly and as fully as I would. Yet I trust in our Lord God almighty that he will, of his goodness and for your love, make you receive it more ghostly and more sweetly than I can or may tell it.

THE TENTH CHAPTER

The second Revelation is of his discolouring, etc.; of our redemption and the discolouring of the vernicle; and how it pleaseth God that we seek him earnestly, waiting on him steadfastly and trusting in him mightily

AND after this I saw, with bodily sight, in the face of the crucifix that hung before me, and upon which I gazed continually, a part of his passion: the contumely, the spitting, the soiling and the buffeting, and many distressful pains—more than I can tell; with a frequent changing of colour. At one time I saw how half the face, beginning from the ear, was covered over with dried blood, ending in the middle of the face; and after that, the other half, in the same way; and between-whiles, the sight of the one side vanished as quickly as it came. This I saw bodily, but with difficulty and obscurely. I desired more bodily light so as to have seen more clearly. And I was answered in my reason: "If God willeth to shew thee more, he shall be thy light; thou needest none but him." For I saw him and sought him.

We are, here, so blind and so unwise that we can never seek God until the time that he of his goodness sheweth himself to us. And when we see something of him, graciously, then are we moved, by this same grace, to seek with a great desire to see him more blissfully. And thus I saw him and I sought him; I had him and I wanted him. This is, and should be, our ordinary working in this life, as I see it.

And now in my understanding I was let down on to the sea-bed. And there I saw hills and dales, green, as though there were moss agrowing amongst the wrack and gravel. Then I understood that even were a man or a woman there under the broad water, if he could have sight of God, even as God is—with a man continually—he would be safe in soul and body, and take no harm. And above and beyond this, he would have more solace and comfort than all this world can or may tell. It is his will that we believe that we see him continually, though it seemeth to us that the sight is but little. And in this belief, he maketh us to get ever more grace. For he will be seen, and he will be sought; he will be waited on and he will be trusted.

This second shewing was so low, so little and so simple that my spirits were in great travail as I beheld in mourning, full of dread and longing. I was for some time in a fear, wondering whether it was a shewing or not. And then, on different occasions our Lord gave me clearer sight whereby I understood truly that it *was* a shewing; that it was a figure and a likeness of our unclean mortal slough, which our fair bright blessed Lord wore for our sins. With its many changes of colour—brown and black, its pitiful and drawn look, it made me think of the holy vernicle of Rome, upon which he imprinted his own blessed face, when he was in his hard passion and going willingly to his death. Of this image many wondered how it could be so, since that he imprinted it with that blessed face which is the fairest in heaven, th flower of the earth and the fruit of the maiden's womb—how could this image be so discoloured and so far from fairness? I desire to say as I have understood it by the grace of God:

We know in our faith and in our belief through the teaching and the preaching of Holy Church that the blissful Trinity made man's kind to his image and likeness. In the same manner, we know that when man fell so deep and so wretchedly by sin, there was no other help to restore man than through him that made man. And he that made man for love, by this same love willed to restore man to the same bliss, and even more. For right as we were made like to the Trinity in our first making, our Maker willed that we should be like to Jesus Christ our Saviour, in heaven without end, by virtue of our again-making. Then between these two makings he willed, for love and for worship of man, to make himself as like to man in this mortal life—in our foulness and in our wretchedness—as a man could be without guilt. Hence the meaning is, as is beforesaid, that it was the image and likeness of our unclean mortal flesh, wherein our fair bright blessed Lord hid his Godhead. Though indeed I dare say, and we ought to believe, that so fair a man was never none but he, until the time that his fair colour was changed with travail and sorrow, passion and dying. Of this it is spoken in the eighth revelation, where it treateth more of the same likeness; the same is said of the vernicle of Rome—that it is alive in its many changes of colour, and its look is sometimes more comfortable and life-like, and sometimes more pitiful and death-like: as may be seen in the eighth revelation.

This vision was a lesson to my understanding, that the continual seeking of the soul pleaseth God much. For it can do no more than seek, suffer and trust; and this is wrought, in every soul that hath it, by the Holy Ghost. But the clearness of the finding—that is of his special grace, whenever it is his will. The seeking with faith, hope and charity pleaseth our Lord; the finding pleaseth the soul and full filleth it with joy. Thus was my understanding taught that seeking is as good as beholding during the time that he willeth to suffer the soul to be in travail. It is God's will that we seek unto the beholding of him; for by that shall he shew us himself, of his special grace whenever he will. And how a soul is to keep herself in the beholding of him, that he shall teach, himself —which is the most worship to him and most profit to the soul, and most cometh of meekness and the virtues, with the grace and the leading of the Holy Ghost. For a soul that simply fasteneth himself to God with true trust, either in seeking or beholding—there is the most worship that he can do, as I see it.

There are two workings that can be seen in this vision: the one is seeking, the other is beholding. The seeking is common—every soul can have that, of his grace, and ought to have it: spiritual discernment and the teaching of Holy Church. It is God's will that we have three things in our seeking, of his gift. The first is that we seek as earnestly and willingly, without sloth, as may be with his grace; and gladly and merrily, without unreasonable heaviness or vain sorrow. The second is that we wait on him steadfastly, for his love, without grudging or striving against him, unto our life's end; for it shall last but a while. The third is that we trust in him mightily, with full and true faith. For it is his will that we know that he shall appear suddenly and blissfully to all his lovers. For his working is secret; but he willeth to be perceived, and his appearing shall be right sudden. He will be trusted, because he is full courteous and homely. Blessed may he be!

THE ELEVENTH CHAPTER

The third Revelation, etc.: How God doeth all things except sin, never changing his purpose, without end; for he hath made all things in the fullness of his goodness

AFTER this, I saw God in a point: the sight, I say, was in my understanding, by which I saw that he is in all things. I beheld with attention, seeing and knowing in it, that he doeth all that is done. (As I saw, I marvelled softly and with dread, and thought: "What is sin?") I saw truly that God doeth all things be they never so little. And I saw truly that nothing is done by hap or by chance, but all by the foreseeing wisdom of God. If a thing be hap or chance according to man's judgement, the cause is our blindness and lack of foreknowledge. For those things that are in the foreseeing wisdom of God from without-beginning, which he rightfully and worshipfully and continually bringeth to their best end, in their coming-about they fall to our notice suddenly and without our knowledge. And thus, because of our blindness and lack of foreknowledge, we say that these things are by hap and by chance. So I understood in this shewing of love, and know well, that in the sight of our Lord God there is neither hap nor chance. Wherefore I needs must grant that all that is done is well done, since our Lord God doeth all.

In this time the working of creatures was not shewed, but only of our Lord God in creatures. For he is in the mid-point of all things, and he doeth all; but I was sure that he doeth no sin. Hence I saw truly that sin is no-deed; for in all this sin was not shewed. Nor would I any longer wonder over this, but simply beheld our Lord and what he willed to shew me. Thus as far as it could be for the time, the rightfulness of God's working was shewed to my soul. Rightfulness hath two fair properties: it is right, and it is full. Even so are all the works of our Lord, they need the working neither of mercy nor of grace; for where nothing faileth all things are rightful. (It was at another time that his shewing concerned the beholding of sin nakedly, and how then he useth the working of mercy and grace: as I shall tell you.)

This vision, then, was shewed to my understanding because it is our Lord's will to have the soul truly turned into the beholding of him, and of all his works as well; for they are full good. All his judgements are easy and sweet, and they bring to great ease the soul that is turned from the beholding of the blind judgement of man into the fair sweet judgement of our Lord God. For man beholdeth some deeds as well done, and some deeds as evil: but our Lord beholdeth them not so. For as all that hath being, in kind, is of God's making, so everything that is done is so in virtue of God's doing. It is easy to understand that the best deed is well done; and just so well done as is the best deed and the highest, even so well done is the least deed; and all according to his attributes, and in the order that our Lord hath ordained it to, from without-beginning: for there is no doer but he. I saw full truly that he changeth never his purpose in any manner of thing, nor ever shall, without end. For there was nothing unknown to him in the rightness of his decrees, from without-beginning. And therefore all things were set in order, ere any thing was made, as they were to stand without end. And no manner thing shall fail in that point; for he hath made all things in the fullness of his goodness.

And therefore the blessed Trinity is ever fully pleased in all his works. All this he shewed me full blissfully, meaning it thus:

See, I am God: see, I am in all things: see, I do all things: see, I never lift my hands off my works, nor ever shall, without end: see, I lead all thing to the end that I ordain it to, from without-beginning, by the same might, wisdom and love that I made it with. How should anything be amiss?

Thus mightily, wisely and lovingly was my soul questioned in this vision; and I saw truly that I needs must assent with great reverence, and have joy in God.

THE TWELFTH CHAPTER

The fourth Revelation, etc.; How it pleaseth God rather and better that we should wash us in his blood, from sin, than in water; for his blood is most precious

AFTER this I saw in my beholding his body bleeding freely in the furrows of the scourging. The fair skin was broken and beaten deep into the tender flesh with the sharp smitings. All about his sweet body the warm blood ran out so freely that there was seen neither skin nor wound, but as it were all blood. And when it came to the point where it should have fallen to the ground, it vanished. Notwithstanding this, the bleeding continued for a while so that it could be seen without doubt; and it was so plenteous, in my sight, that had it really been blood, in kind and in substance, at that time, it would have saturated all the bed, and have spread all about—so it seemed to me.

Then it came to my mind that God hath made the waters of earth plenteous for our service and bodily refreshment, of the tender love that he hath to us. But yet it pleaseth him better that we should use, full homely, his blessed blood to wash us clean from sin. For there is no liquor made, which it pleaseth him so well to give us. For as it is most plenteous, so it is most precious; and that by the power of the blessed Godhead. It is of our own kind, and all blissfully floweth over us by the power of his precious love. This very dear blood of our Lord Jesus Christ, as truly as it is most precious, so truly it is most plenteous. Behold and see the power of this precious plenty of his most dear blood. It descended down into hell, and delivered all those there that belong to the court of heaven, breaking their bonds. The precious plenty of his most dear blood floweth over all the earth, and is at hand to wash clean from sin all creatures of good will, who are, have been and shall be. The precious plenty of his most dear blood ascendeth up into heaven, in the blessed body of our Lord Jesus Christ. It is flowing in him, praying for us to the Father; and so it is and shall be, as long as we have need. And ever more it floweth in all heaven, rejoicing in the salvation of all man's kind that are there and shall be, unto the fulfilment of the number that is wanting.

THE THIRTEENTH CHAPTER

The fifth Revelation sheweth that the temptation of the fiend is overcome by the passion of Christ; to the increase of joy in us, and to the fiend's pain, everlastingly

AFTERWARDS, before God shewed any words, he permitted me to behold in him, for a suitable time, all that I had seen and all the understanding that was therein, so far as the simpleness of my soul could take it. Then, without voice or opening of lips, he formed in my soul these words: "Herewith is the fiend overcome." This word our Lord said, meaning his blessed passion which he had just shewed.

In this our Lord shewed a part of the fiend's malice and the fullness of his unmight. For he shewed that his passion is the overcoming of the fiend. God shewed that the fiend hath now the same malice that he had before the incarnation. And as sorely as he travaileth, even so continually he seeth that all souls belonging to salvation escape him, worshipfully, by the power of his precious passion. That is his sorrow; and most evilly is he afflicted. For all that God suffereth him to do turneth to our joy, and to his shame and pain. And he hath as much sorrow when God giveth him leave to work as when he worketh not; and that is because he can never do the ill that he would. For his might is all locked in God's hand. And though in God there can be no wrath, as I see it, yet our good Lord, having endless regard to his own worship and to the profit of all them that shall be saved, with might and right withstandeth the reprobate, who in their malice and frowardness busy themselves to be contrary, and act against God's will.

Also I saw our Lord scorning his malice and bringing to naught his might; and he wills that we do likewise. At this sight I laughed mightily—which made them laugh that were about me. And their laughter was a liking to me; and I thought, "Would that all my even-christians had seen as I saw; then would they all have laughed with me." But I saw not Christ laughing—it was the sight that he shewed me, I well know, that made me to laugh. Yet I understood that we may laugh both for comfort of ourselves and in our rejoicing in God. For the fiend is overcome.

(This sight, where I saw him scorn the fiend's malice, was by the fastening of my understanding inwardly to our Lord; that is to say, an inward shewing of his truth, in his unchanging expression. This, as I see it, is a worshipful attribute of his—to be immutable.)

Then I fell into more serious mood, and said to myself: "I see three things, game, scorn and earnest. I see a game in which the fiend is overcome; I see scorn, in that God scorneth him, and he shall be scorned; and I see an earnest, in that he is overcome by the blissful passion and death of our Lord Jesus Christ, which was done in full great earnest."

And where I said "he is scorned", I meant that God scorneth him; that is to say, he seeth him now as he shall do without-end. For in this God shewed that the fiend is damned—which I meant when I said that he should be scorned. For I saw that he shall be scorned at doomsday, generally, by all that shall be saved—those of whose salvation he hath had great envy. For then he shall see that all the woe and tribulation he hath done shall be turned into increase of their joy without end. And all the pain and the sorrow he would have brought them to shall go with him to hell, for ever.

THE FOURTEENTH CHAPTER

The sixth Revelation is of the worshipful thanks with which he rewardeth his servants, and it hath three joys

AFTER this, our Lord said: "I thank thee for thy service, and for the travail of thy youth." And in this my understanding was lifted up into heaven, where I saw our Lord God as a Lord in his own house—a Lord who hath called all his most dear friends to a solemn feast. Then I saw the Lord taking no seat in his own house; but I saw him royally reigning in his house, filling it all full with joy and mirth, himself, endlessly: to bring gladness and solace to his most dear friends, full homely and full courteously, with a marvellous melody of endless love in his own fair blissful countenance: for the shining countenance of the Godhead filleth all heaven full of joy and bliss.

God shewed three degrees of bliss that each soul shall have in heaven that hath willingly served God in any degree in earth. The first is the worshipful thanks of our Lord God that he shall receive when he is delivered out of pain. This thanks is so high and so worshipful that it seemeth that it would fill him even if he received no more. For, methought, all the pain and travail that all living men might suffer could not have deserved the worshipful thanks that one man shall have who willingly shall have served God. The second is that all the blessed creatures that are in heaven shall see this worshipful thanking—he maketh the service of him known to all that are in heaven. When a king thanketh his subjects it is great worship to them; but if he maketh it known to all the realm, then their worship is much increased. The third is that as new and as pleasing as the thanks is when it is first received, even so shall it last without end. And I saw how homely and sweetly was this shewed—that the age of every man shall be known in heaven, and he shall be rewarded for the time of his willing service. And especially the age of them that willingly and freely offer their youth is surpassingly rewarded and wonderfully thanked. But I saw that whenever or what time a man or woman be truly turned to God for one day's service according to his endless will, they shall have all these three degrees of bliss. And the more that the loving soul seeth this courtesy of God, the more eager she is to serve him all her life.

THE FIFTEENTH CHAPTER

The seventh Revelation is of our oftentimes feeling weal and woe; and how it is expedient that a man sometimes be left without comfort, even when sin is not the cause

AFTER this he shewed a sovereign ghostly liking in my soul. In this liking I was filled full of everlasting sureness, mightily fastened in me, with absence of all painful dread. This was so glad and so ghostly a feeling that I was all in peace, in ease and in rest, so that there was nothing in earth that might have grieved me. Yet it lasted only for a while; and then I was left to myself, feeling the heaviness and weariness of life, and irksomeness of myself; so that I scarcely had patience to live. There was neither comfort nor ease as far as feelings go; only faith, hope and charity—and in truth I had these but little in feeling. But soon enough after this, our Lord gave me again the comfort and rest of soul, the liking and the sureness, so blissfully and so mightily that no dread nor any sorrow, nor pain bodily or ghostly that I might possibly experience, could have diseased me. And then I experienced again the pain; and then the liking; and now the one, and now the other, divers times—I suppose about twenty times. In the time of the joy I could have said with St Paul: "Nothing shall part me from the charity of Christ". And in the pain, I could have said with St Peter: "Lord, save me, I perish".

This vision was shewed to my understanding to teach me that it is expedient to some souls to have experience in this wise—sometimes to be in comfort, and sometimes to lack comfort and to be left to themselves. It is God's will that we know that he keepeth us surely, ever the same, in woe and in weal; and that for profit of his soul a man is sometimes left to himself, without his sin always being the cause. For in this time I had not sinned so as to be left to myself; also it was all so sudden. I did not deserve, either, to have the blessed feelings. Our Lord giveth them freely, when so he will; and sometimes suffereth us to be in woe. And both are the one love. It is God's will that we keep us in comfort with all our might. For bliss is lasting without end; whilst pain is passing, and shall be brought to naught in them that shall be saved. Therefore it is not God's will that we keep step with our feeling of pains, by sorrowing and mourning for them; but rather at once pass them over, and keep ourselves in the endless liking which is God.

THE SIXTEENTH CHAPTER

The eighth Revelation is of the last piteous pains of Christ's dying, and the discolouring of his face, and the drying of his flesh

AFTER this Christ shewed me the part of his passion near his death. I saw his sweet face as it was then, dry and bloodless with the pallor of a dying man: deathly pale with the anguish. The pallor became more death-like, first taking a bluish tinge; and then, as death affected the flesh more deeply, a brownish blue. His passion was shewed to me essentially in his blessed face—wherein I saw these four colours—and particularly in his lips, which were before a fresh and vivid red, pleasing to the sight. This changing colour in his dying was pitiful to see. And also, as I gazed, his nostrils were clogged and dried, and his sweet body became brown and then black—the fair, fresh and lively colour of him changed and turned by the fever into this dying dryness. For in that time that our Saviour died upon the Rood, there was a sharp dry wind—I saw it—dreadfully cold. And when all the precious blood that could flow from his blessed body was bled out, there yet remained a moisture in the sweet flesh of Christ. But the loss of blood and the pain within, and the blowing of the wind and the cold from without, met together in the sweet body of Christ; these four dried up the flesh of Christ as time went on. The pain, sharp and bitter as it was, was yet long-lasting—I saw it. And the pain dried up all the lively quality of Christ's flesh. So I saw the sweet flesh dry before my eyes, part by part, and with marvellous pain. As long as there was spirit and life in Christ's flesh, so long suffered he. This pain seemed to last as long as if he had been seven nights in death, dying all the time, at the very point of passing away, and suffering always this great pain. Where I say "it seemed . . . as if he had been seven nights in death", this specifieth that his sweet body was so discoloured, so dry, so shrunken, so death-like and so piteous as though he had been seven nights in death, dying all the time. And methought that the drying of Christ's flesh was the greatest pain, and the last, of his passion.

THE SEVENTEENTH CHAPTER

Of the grievous bodily thirst of Christ, and its fourfold cause; of his piteous crowning, and of what giveth most pain to a true lover of his

IN this drying there was brought to my mind the word that Christ said: "I thirst". I saw in Christ a double thirst: the one, bodily, the other, ghostly. This was shewed me for the bodily thirst; what was shewed me for the ghostly thirst, I shall tell afterwards.

By the bodily thirst I understood that the moisture in the body failed; for the blessed flesh and bones were left all alone without blood or moisture. The body was drying up an exceeding long time, through the wounds caused by the nails and the weight of the body. For I perceived that because of the tenderness of his sweet hands and feet, and the size and grievous hardness of the nails, the wounds grew wider as the body constantly sagged by its weight in the long hanging. And in the beginning, whilst the flesh was still fresh and bleeding, the continual pressure of the thorns widened the wounds, caused by the piercing and tearing of the head in the binding-in of the crown (I saw it all baked with dry blood, with the sweet hair tangling the dry flesh amongst the thorns, and the thorns amidst the flesh as it dried). I saw further that the sweet skin and the tender flesh, mingled with hair and blood, had been prised loose from the bone by the thorns, and broken in many pieces; which were hanging down, and would have fallen away had there still been natural moisture. (I saw not how this came about, but I understood that it was because of the sharp thorns.) The rough and grievous binding-on of the garland, unsparing and pitiless, had broken all the sweet skin and flesh—yea, and loosened it from the bone; it was torn in strips like a cloth, hanging down, and with its looseness and weight like to have fallen. This was great sorrow and fear to me; for methought I would not for my life have seen it fall.

This sight continued a while; then it began to change. I looked, and wondered—was it possible? Then I saw it was; for it began to dry and lose a part of the weight. The garland of thorns was dyed with the blood that was round about the garland—so that it was covered all round, like one garland on another. And this second garland [of blood] and the head were all one colour, the colour of clotted blood when it drieth. The skin of the flesh of his face and body that shewed was a little wrinkled, and of a tawny colour—the colour of dry board when it is old; and the face was browner than the body.

I saw four reasons for the drying. The first was the loss of blood: the second, the pain which accompanied it: the third is that he was hanging up in the air as men hang out a cloth to dry: the fourth, that his bodily kind demanded drink, and there was no manner of comfort ministered to him. Hard and grievous was that pain. But much harder and more grievous it was when the moisture failed, and all the flesh began to dry and shrink. These were two pains that shewed in the blessed head. The first (the loss of blood) worked the drying whilst the flesh was moist. The second was a drawn-out pain, with the shrinking and the drying through the blowing of the wind from without; this dried him more and pained him with more than my heart can think, more than all his other pains: concerning which, I saw that all that I can say is too little; they cannot be told.

The shewing of Christ's pains filled me full of pain. For though I knew well that he had suffered just the once; yet he wished to shew me his pain and fill me with mind of it, as I had before desired of him. In all this time of Christ's presence, I felt no pain except for Christ's pain. Then it seemed I knew but little what his pain was that I had asked for; and like a wretch I repented me—thinking that had I known what it was like, I would have been loath to pray for it. For my pain seemed to pass beyond any bodily death; and I thought: "Is any pain in hell like this?" And I was answered in my reason: "Hell is a different pain, for there is despair." Of all the pains that lead to salvation, this is the greatest—to see the Lover suffer. How could any pain be greater than to see him, that is all my life, all my bliss and all my joy, suffer? Here felt I steadfastly that I loved Christ so much above myself that there was no pain that could be suffered like to the sorrow I had, to see him in pain.

THE EIGHTEENTH CHAPTER

Of the Spiritual Martyrdom of our Lady and other lovers of Christ; and how all things, good and ill, suffered with him

HERE I saw, in part, the compassion of our blessed Lady Saint Mary, for Christ. She was so oned to him in love, that the greatness of her love was cause of the greatness of her pain. In this I saw the substance of the kind love his creatures have to him, continued by grace. Which kind love was most abundantly shewed in his sweet Mother—an overpassing love. For as much as she loved him more than any other, even so her pain surpassed all others. For ever the higher, the mightier and the sweeter that the love is, the more sorrow it is to the lover to see that body that he loves, in pain. And so all his disciples and all his true lovers suffered more pain than in their own bodily dying. For I am sure, in my own feeling, that the least of them loved him so far above themselves that it passeth all that I can say.

Here I saw, in my understanding, a great oneing between Christ and us. For when he was in pain, we were in pain; and all creatures that could suffer pain, suffered with him; that is to say, all creatures that God hath made for our service. Heaven and earth failed in their kind for sorrow at Christ's dying. For it belongeth to their kindly property to recognize as their Lord, him in whom all their virtue standeth. And when he failed, then needs must they, for kindness, fail with him in as much as they could, in sorrow for his pains. Thus those that were his friends suffered pain, for love; and all in general suffered. That is to say: they that knew him not, suffered in the failing of every manner of comfort except in the mighty secret keeping of God. I speak of two sorts of people that knew him not—as may be understood by these two persons, one, Pilate; the other St Denis of France, who was at that time a pagan. For when he saw the wonders and marvels, the sorrows and dreads that befell in that time, he said: "Either the world is now at an end, or else he that is Maker of Kind is suffering". Wherefore he wrote on an altar: "This is the altar of the unknown God". It is God, of his goodness, that maketh the planets and the elements to work in their kind for both the blessed and the cursed; in that time this working was withdrawn from both. Wherefore it was that they who knew him not were in sorrow in that time.

Thus was our Lord Jesus pained for us; and we all stand in this way of pain, with him, and shall do until we come to his bliss; as I shall say hereafter.

THE NINETEENTH CHAPTER

Of the comfortable beholding of the crucifix; and how the desire of the flesh without consent of the soul is no sin, and the flesh must be in pain, suffering until both be oned to Christ

IN this time I would have looked away from the cross; yet I durst not. For I knew well that whilst I beheld the cross I was sure and safe; therefore I would not consent to put my soul in peril. For apart from the cross was no surety against the fears of fiends. Then I had an offer in my reason; it was said to me, as though by a friend: "Look up to heaven to his Father". Then through the faith that I felt I saw well that there was nothing between the cross and heaven that could have dis-eased me. Here then I must needs look up, or else answer. So I answered inwardly, with all the might of my soul, and said: "Nay, I cannot, for Thou art my heaven". This I said because I would not. For I would rather have been in that pain till doomsday than have come to heaven otherwise than by him. For I knew well that he who had bound me so sore, would unbind me when he would.

Thus was I taught to choose Jesus for my heaven, whom I saw at that time only in pain. No other heaven pleased me than Jesus, who shall be my bliss when I come there. And this hath ever been a comfort to me, that I chose Jesus, by his grace, to be my heaven in all this time of passion and sorrow. And that hath been a lesson to me that I should evermore do so—choose only Jesus to be my heaven, in weal and in woe. And though, as I said before, like a wretch I felt regret—if I had known what the pain was to be, I would have been loath to pray for it; yet here I saw truly that this was merely the grumbling and frailty of the flesh without the consent of the soul, to which God assigneth no blame. Feeling of regret and wilful choice are two contraries both of which I had at that time; they are two parts, an outward and an inward. The outward part is our mortal flesh which is now in pain and woe, and shall be, in this life; of which I felt much in this time. The inward part is a high and a blessed life which is all in peace and in love; and this is more secretly felt. It was in this part that mightily, wisely and willingly I chose Jesus to be my heaven.

In this I saw truly that the inward part is the master and sovereign of the outward, neither censuring nor taking heed of its desire; but all the intent of the will is set endlessly to be oned to our Lord Jesus. That the outward part could draw the inward to its own assent—this was not shewed to me; but that the inward part, by grace, draweth the outward part, and both shall be oned in bliss without end by the power of Christ—this was shewed.

THE TWENTIETH CHAPTER

Of the ineffable passion of Christ, and of three things of the passion always to be remembered

THUS I saw our Lord Jesus languishing a long time: for the oneing with the Godhead gave strength to the manhood to suffer, for love, more than all the rest of men might suffer. I mean not only more pain than all men might suffer, but also that he suffered more pain than all men of salvation that ever were from the first beginning unto the last day could tell of or fully reckon; having regard to the worthiness of this highest worshipful King and his shameful ignominious death. For he that is highest and worthiest was most foully condemned and utterly despised. For the highest point to be seen in his passion is to consider and to know that it is God that suffered; seeing, after this, two points which are lower.

One is, what he suffered: and the other, for whom he suffered.

In this he brought to my mind, in part, the high nobility of the glorious Godhead, and therewith the preciousness and the tender nature of his blessed body—which are oned together; and also the loathfulness that there is in our kind to suffer pain. For as he was most sensitively and perfectly formed, right so he was most strong and mighty to suffer. And for the sins of every man that shall be saved he suffered; and he saw and endured every man's sorrow, desolation and anguish, in his kindness and love. For in as much as our Lady sorrowed for his pains, as much suffered he sorrow for her sorrows—and more: as much more as his sweet manhood is worthier in kind. As long as he was passible, he suffered for us. And now he is uprisen and no more passible, yet still he suffereth with us, as I shall say afterwards.

I, beholding all this by his grace, saw that the love which he hath to our soul was so strong in him that wilfully he chose his passion with great desire; and meekly he suffered it with great joy. The soul that beholdeth this when touched by his grace shall truly see that these pains of Christ's passion pass all other pains; and that all these other pains shall be turned into everlasting joy by the power of Christ's passion. It is God's will, as I understand it, that we have three manners of beholding of his blessed passion; the first of which is the severe pain that he suffered, with contrition and compassion. That shewed our Lord in this time, and gave me the power and the grace to see it.

THE TWENTY-FIRST CHAPTER

How we are now dying on the cross with Christ; but his looking on us putteth away all our pain

I LOOKED for the going forth of the soul with all my might, and thought to have seen his body wholly dead. But I saw him not so. For just at the time that it seemed to me his life could no longer last, and that the shewing of his end must needs be nigh, suddenly (I still beheld the cross) his blessed face changed. This change in him changed me, and I was as glad and merry as it is possible to be. Then our Lord brought to my mind these joyful words: "Where now is any trace of thy pain or of thy anguish?" And I was full of joy. I understood that in this life, as our Lord sees it, we are on his cross, dying with him in our pains and our passion. Then suddenly his countenance shall be changed upon us, and we shall be with him in heaven. Between this disposition and the other there shall be no break in time—and then we shall all be brought into joy. (Thus meant he in shewing these words: "Where now is any trace of thy pain or of thy grief?") And we shall be full of bliss.

Here saw I truly that if he shewed now to us his blessed face, there is no pain in earth nor in any other place that could trouble us, but all things would be to us joy and bliss. But because he sheweth us the dispositions of his passion which he bore in this life—his cross, therefore we are in dis-ease and travail with him, as our kind demandeth. And the reason why he suffereth is that he willeth, of his goodness, to make us heirs with him in his bliss. And in return for this little pain that we suffer here, we shall have an endless high knowing in God, which we could never have without it. And the more severe our pains shall have been with him in his cross, the greater shall our worship be with him in his kingdom.

THE TWENTY-SECOND CHAPTER

The ninth Revelation is of the liking, etc.; of three heavens and the infinite love of Christ in his desiring every day to suffer for us, if he could; although it is not needful

THEN said our good Lord, asking: "Art thou well paid that I suffered for thee?" I said: "Yea good Lord, by thy mercy: yea, good Lord, blessed mayest thou be." Then said Jesus, our good Lord: "If thou art paid, I am paid. It is a joy, a bliss and an endless liking to me that ever I suffered passion for thee. And if I could suffer more, I would suffer more."

Whilst I experienced this, my understanding was lifted up into heaven; and there I saw three heavens. At this sight I greatly marvelled, and thought: "I see three heavens, and all are of the blessed manhood of Christ; and no one of them is greater, no one is less: no one is higher, no one is lower: but all are equal in blessedness." As for the first heaven, Christ shewed me his Father—not in bodily likeness, but in his Fatherhood and in his working: that is to say, I saw in Christ that the Father is. The working of the Father is this: —that he giveth a prize to his Son, Jesus Christ. This gift, this prize is so blissful to Jesus, that his Father could not have given him a prize that would have pleased him better. The first heaven is his pleasing of the Father (it was shewed me as a heaven, for it was full of blessedness). For the Father is well pleased with all the deeds that Jesus has done concerning our salvation. Wherefore we are not only his by his buying, but also, by the courteous gift of his Father, we are his bliss, we are his prize, we are his worship, we are his crown.

This was a singular source of wonder, and a beholding full of delight—that we should be his crown. It is, as I say, so great a bliss to Jesus that he setteth at naught his travail and his passion and his cruel and shameful death.

In these words, "if I could suffer more I would suffer more", I saw truly that as often as he could die, so often he would: and love would never let him have rest until he had done it. And I looked with great diligence to see how often he would die if he could. And truly, the number so far surpassed my understanding and my wits, that my reason might not or could not comprehend it or take it in. And suppose he had thus often died or were to die, even then he would set it at naught, for love. For though the sweet manhood of Christ could suffer but once, the goodness of him can never cease to repeat the offer: every day, he is ready for the same, if it were possible. If he had said that he would, for my love, make new heavens and new earths, that were of little account—he could do this every day, if he would, without any travail; but to die for my love, so often that the number surpasses a creature's reason—that is the highest offer that our Lord God could make to man's soul, as I see it. His meaning then is this:

> How could it be, then, that I would not do, for thy love, all the things in my power which trouble me not to do: seeing that I would wish, for thy love, to die so often—having no regard for my hard pains.

And here saw I concerning the second heaven, as I beheld his blessed passion: the love that made him to suffer passeth so far above all his pain as heaven is above earth. For the pain was a noble, precious and worshipful deed done in time, by the working of love. But the love was without beginning, is, and shall be without end. In this love he said most sweetly this word, "if I could suffer more, I would suffer more". He said not "if it were needful to suffer more", but "if I could suffer more". For even though it were not needful, if he could suffer more, he would.

This deed and this work concerning our salvation was

ordained as well as God could ordain it. It was done as worshipfully as Christ could do it. Herein I saw fullness of bliss in Christ; for his bliss would not have been full, if it could any better have been done than it was done.

THE TWENTY-THIRD CHAPTER

How Christ willeth that we rejoice with him greatly in our redemption, and that we desire grace from him that we may so do

IN these three words, "it is a joy, a bliss and an endless liking to me", were shewed three heavens—thus: for the joy, I understood the good pleasure of the Father: for the bliss, the worship of the Son: and for the endless liking, the Holy Ghost. The Father is pleased, the Son is worshipped, the Holy Ghost liketh.

And here saw I concerning the third heaven as I beheld his blessed passion: that is to say, the joy and the bliss that maketh him to like it. For our courteous Lord shewed his passion to me in five manners; of which the first is the bleeding of the head: the second is the discolouring of his blessed face: the third is the plenteous bleeding of the body as it was in the scourging: the fourth is the deep drying. These four, as hath been said before, were shewed as the pains of the passion. The fifth is this that was shewed as the joy and bliss of the passion. For it is God's will that we have true liking, with him, of our salvation; and he willeth that we be mightily comforted and strengthened therein; and he willeth that our soul be thus happily occupied, with his grace. For we are his bliss, and in us he hath liking without end; and so shall we have in him, with his grace. All that he doeth for us, and has done and ever shall do, was never cost nor expense to him, except when he died in our manhood. Beginning at the sweet incarnation, and lasting till the blessed uprising on Easter morrow—just so long endured the cost and the expense of the deed of our redemption. In this deed he ever rejoiceth, endlessly, as is before said.

Jesus willeth that we take heed of this bliss that is in the blessed Trinity concerning our salvation; and that we desire to have the same ghostly liking, as is before said. That is to say, our liking in our salvation should be like to the joy that Christ hath in our salvation, as much as may be whilst we are here. All the Trinity worked in the passion of Christ, ministering an abundance of power and plenty of grace to us by him. But only the Maiden's Son suffered. Whereof all the blessed Trinity rejoiceth. This was shewed in the word, "Art thou well paid", and in the other word that Christ said, "if thou art well paid, I am well paid"; as if he had said: "It is joy and liking enough to me, and I ask naught else from thee for my travail but that I might pay thee well."

In this he brought to my mind the proper quality of a glad giver. A glad giver ever taketh but little heed of the thing that he giveth; all his desire and all his intent is to please and to solace him to whom he giveth it. And if the receiver take the gift gladly and thankfully, then the courteous giver setteth at naught all his cost and all his labour, in return for the joy and delight that he hath; for he hath pleased and solaced him that he loveth. Plenteously and fully was this shewed.

Think also wisely of the greatness of this word *ever*. For in it was shewed a high knowing of the love that Christ hath of our salvation, with the manifold joys that follow out of his passion. One is, he rejoiceth that he hath done it in deed, and shall no more suffer. Another is that he hath therewith bought us from the endless pains of hell. Another is that he hath brought us up into heaven, and hath made us to be his crown and his endless bliss.

THE TWENTY-FOURTH CHAPTER

The tenth Revelation is our Lord Jesus shewing in love his blessed heart cloven in two, rejoicing

With a glad countenance our good Lord looked into his side, and beheld with joy. And with his sweet looking he led forth the understanding of his creature through this same wound into his side. And there, within, he shewed a fair and delightful place, large enough for all mankind that shall be saved to rest there, in peace and in love. Therewith he brought to my mind the most dear blood and precious water which he let pour out for love. In his sweet beholding he shewed his blessed heart cloven in two; and in his sweet enjoying he shewed to my understanding, in part, the blissful Godhead—as far forth as he would at that time, and strengthening the poor soul to understand, so to say, the endless love that was without beginning and is and shall be ever. For with this our good Lord said, most blissfully, "Lo how I love thee". As if he had said: "My darling behold and see thy Lord, thy God, that is thy Maker and thine endless joy; see thine own Brother, thy Saviour; my child, behold and see what liking and what bliss I have in thy salvation; and for love of me, rejoice with me." To still more understanding was said this blessed word, "Lo how I love thee". As if he had said:

> Behold and see that I loved thee so much (before ever I died for thee) that I would die for thee. And now I have died for thee, and have suffered as willingly as I may. And now is all my bitter pain and all my hard travail turned to

my everlasting joy and bliss. And as to thee, how should it now be that thou shouldst anything pray me that pleaseth me, and that I should not full gladly grant it thee? For my pleasure is thy holiness and thine endless joy and bliss with me.

This is the understanding that I had, said as simply as I can, of this blessed word, "Lo how I loved thee". This shewed our good Lord to make us glad and merry.

THE TWENTY-FIFTH CHAPTER

The eleventh Revelation is a high ghostly shewing of his Mother

HIS countenance full of this mirth and joy, our Lord looked down on the right side and brought to my mind our Lady, and where she stood during the time of his passion; and said, "Wilt thou see her?" In this sweet word it was as if he had said:

> I know well that thou wilt see my blessed Mother; for after myself she is the highest joy that I might shew thee; she is the most liking and worship to me, and of all my blessed creatures sight of her is most desired.

Out of the marvellous high and special love that he hath for this sweet maiden his blessed Mother, our Lady Saint Mary, he sheweth her bliss and joy—such is the meaning of this sweet word. It was as if he said, "Wilt thou see how I love her so that thou mightest joy with me in the love that I have in her, and she in me?"

This sweet word our good Lord speaketh in love to all mankind that shall be saved (for our greater understanding) as it were to one person. It is as if he said: "Wilt thou see in her how thou art loved? For thy love I have made her so high, so noble and so worthy. This liketh me, and so will I that it do thee."

After himself, she is the most blissful sight. Yet because of this I am not taught to long to see her bodily presence whilst I am here, but only the virtues of her blessed soul, her truth, her wisdom, her charity; whereby I am taught to know myself and reverently to dread my God.

When our good Lord had shewed this, and said this word, "Wilt thou see her?" I answered and said, "Yea, good Lord, by thy mercy; yea, good Lord, if it be thy will". Oftentimes I prayed for this; and I thought I might see her in bodily likeness; but I saw her not so. For Jesus in that word shewed me a ghostly sight of her. And just as before I had seen her little and simple, now he shewed her high and noble and glorious, and pleasing to him above all creatures. Even so he willeth it to be known that all those who have liking in him should have liking in her—in the same liking that he hath in her and she in him. It was for greater understanding of this that he shewed this example: if a man love one creature especially and above all creatures, he will make all other creatures to love and to like that creature that he loveth so much. This word that Jesus said "wilt thou see her?" seemed to me the most liking word that he could give me of her—together with the ghostly shewing that he gave me of her. Our Lord shewed me no individual person except our Lady Saint Mary; but her he shewed three times: the first, as she was when she conceived: the second, as she was in her sorrow under the Cross: the third, as she is now, in liking, worship and joy.

THE TWENTY-SIXTH CHAPTER

The twelfth Revelation is that our Lord God is sovereign Being

AFTER this our Lord shewed himself more glorified (if I saw aright) than I had seen him before. Wherein I was taught that our soul shall never have rest till it come into him, knowing that he is fullness of joy, homely, courteous and blissful: true life. Oftentimes our Lord said:

> I it am, I it am; I it am that is highest; I it am that thou lovest; I it am that thou likest; I it am that thou servest; I it am that thou longest; I it am that thou desirest; I it am that thou meanest; I it am that is all; I it am that Holy Church preacheth and teacheth thee; I it am that shewed myself to thee here.

The number of his words passeth beyond my wits, and all my understanding, and all my powers; and they are the highest, as I see it. For therein is comprehended—I cannot tell what: except that the joy that I saw in the shewing of them passeth all that heart can think or soul could desire. Therefore these words are written here only that every man may receive them in our Lord's meaning, according to the grace of understanding and loving that God giveth him.

THE TWENTY-SEVENTH CHAPTER

The thirteenth Revelation is that our Lord God willeth that we have great regard to all the deeds that he hath done—to the great nobleness that belongeth to the making of all things; and how sin is not known except by the pain

AFTER this our Lord brought to my mind the great longing

that I had for him before. And I saw that nothing hindered me but sin; I beheld the same in us all in general. And it occurred to me that if sin had never been, we should all be clean and as like to our Lord as when he made us. Thus in my folly, even before this time, I often wondered why the beginning of sin was not prevented by the great foreseeing wisdom of God; for then—or so it seemed to me—all would have been well. Such a thought was much to be forsaken; yet nevertheless mourning and sorrow I made on this account, without any understanding or spiritual discernment. But Jesus, who in this vision informed me of all that I needed, answered with this word saying: "Sin must needs be, but all shall be well. All shall be well; and all manner thing shall be well."

In this naked word *sin* our Lord brought to my mind, in a general way, all that is not good: the shameful despising and the uttermost tribulation that he bore for us in this life, his dying and all his pains: and the suffering, bodily and ghostly, of all his creatures—for we are all partly brought to naught, and shall be so, following our Master Jesus, until we are fully purged (that is to say, until we are fully brought to naught) in regard of our mortal flesh, and of all those inward affections of ours which are not very good. I beheld this, with all the pains that ever were or ever shall be. (And with all this I understood that the passion of Christ was the greatest and all-surpassing pain.) All this was shewed in a moment; and it quickly changed over to comforting. For our good Lord would not that the soul be afraid of this ugly sight.

And yet I saw not sin. For I believe it hath no manner of substance nor particle of being. It cannot be known except by the pain that is caused thereby. This pain is something, if I see it aright, existing for a time. For it purgeth us, and maketh us to know ourselves and ask mercy; for the passion of our Lord is our comfort against all this—and such is his blessed will. And for the tender love that our good Lord hath to all that shall be saved, he comfortcth them swiftly and sweetly, meaning thus: "It is true that sin is the cause of all this pain. But all shall be well and all shall be well, and all manner thing shall be well." These words were said most tenderly; they shewed no manner of blame either to me or to any that shall be. Hence it would be a great unkindness in me to blame or to wonder at God because of my sin, since he blameth not me for sin.

In these same words I saw a high marvellous secret hid in God—a secret which he shall openly make known to us in heaven. In this knowing we shall truly see the cause why he permitted sin to come. And in this sight we shall endlessly have joy.

THE TWENTY-EIGHTH CHAPTER

How the children of salvation shall be shaken in sorrows, but Christ rejoiceth therein with compassion; of a remedy against tribulation

THUS I saw how Christ hath compassion on us because of sin. And just as I was before, in the passion of Christ, filled full of pain and compassion, so in this I was, in part, filled with compassion for all my even-christians. (For full well he loveth the people that shall be saved—that is to say, God's servants.) Holy Church shall be shaken with sorrow and anguish and tribulation in this world, as men shake a cloth in the wind. But to this our Lord answered in this manner: "A great thing I shall make of this in heaven—a thing of endless worship and of everlasting joy"; so much so that our Lord, as I saw, rejoiceth in the tribulations of his servants, but with pity and compassion. On every person that he loveth, in order to bring them to his bliss, he layeth something, which, though it is of no offence in his sight, is a reason why they are humbled and despised in this world, scorned and mocked and cast out. This he doeth to prevent their taking harm of the pomp and of the pride and of the vainglory of this wretched life, and to make ready the way for them to come to heaven in bliss that shall last without end. For he says: "I shall wholly break you of your vain affections and your vicious pride; and after that I shall gather you and make you meek and mild, clean and holy by oneing you to me." And then I saw that all the kind compassion that a man hath for his even-christians, with charity—this is Christ in him.

The same being brought to naught that he shewed in his passion—it was shewed again here, in this compassion; wherein were two manners of understanding according to our Lord's meaning. One was of the bliss to which we are brought, wherein he willeth that we have joy; the other is, of the comfort in our pain—that we may know that it all shall turn to our worship and our profit by virtue of his passion; and that we may know that we suffered right naught alone, but with him; that we may see him, our ground; and that we may see that his pains and his tribulation so far surpass all that we might suffer, that it cannot be fully comprehended.

The beholding of this will save us from complaint and despair in feeling our pains. And though we see truly that our sins deserve them, yet his love excuseth us. Of his great courtesy he doeth away with all our blame, and beholdeth us with ruth and pity, as children innocent and lovable.

THE TWENTY-NINTH CHAPTER

Adam's sin was the greatest; but the satisfaction for it is more pleasing to God than ever the sin was harmful

But meanwhile I still remained, as I beheld, in sorrow and mourning, saying thus to our Lord—but meaning it with very great dread: "Ah, good Lord, but how can all be well in face of the great harm that is come by sin to thy creatures?" Here I desired, as much as I durst, to have some more open declaring, wherewith I could be eased in this perplexity. And to this our blessed Lord answered most meekly and with a lovely look. He shewed that Adam's sin was the greatest harm that ever was done or ever shall be, unto the world's end. And also he shewed that this is clearly known in all Holy Church on earth. Furthermore he taught me that I should behold the glorious remedy. For this making amends is more pleasing to God and worshipful unto man's salvation, without comparison, than ever was the sin of Adam harmful. Hence our blessed Lord meaneth thus—and in his teaching we must take heed of it: "Seeing that I have made well the greatest harm, it is my will that thou shouldst know thereby that I shall make well all that is less".

THE THIRTIETH CHAPTER

How we should have joy and trust in our Saviour, not presuming to know his secret counsels

He gave understanding of two parts of his truth. One part is our Saviour and our Salvation. This blessed part is open, clear and fair, and light and plenteous. For all mankind that are and shall be of good will are comprehended in this part.

Herein we are bound and drawn to God, and counselled and taught, inwardly by the Holy Ghost and outwardly by Holy Church through the same grace. In this our Lord willeth that we should be occupied—having joy in him: for he hath joy in us. The more plenteously we accept this joy, with reverence and meekness, the more thanks we deserve of him, and the more progress we ourselves make. Thus we may see and enjoy.

This our part is our Lord. The other is hidden and closed to us—that is, all that belongeth not to our salvation. For that is our Lord's secret counsel. It belongeth to the royal Lordship of God to hold his secret counsels in peace. And it belongeth to his servants, out of obedience and reverence, not to wish to know his counsels. Yet our Lord hath pity and compassion on us in that some creatures make themselves so busy therein. And I am sure that if we knew how greatly we would please him, and ease ourselves by leaving it alone, we would do so. The saints in heaven refuse to know anything but what our Lord willeth to shew them. And also their charity and their desires are ruled according to the will of our Lord. And thus ought we to will—that our will be like to theirs. Then should we nothing will, nothing desire but the will of our Lord—just as they do. (For we are all one in God's meaning.) Here was I taught that we should have joy only in our blessed Saviour Jesus, and trust in him for all things.

THE THIRTY-FIRST CHAPTER

Of the longing and the spiritual thirst of Christ, which lasteth and shall last until doomsday; and by reason of his body, he is not yet fully glorified, nor all impassible

Thus our good Lord answered all the questions and doubts that I could bring up, saying for full comfort: "I may make all things well: and I can make all things well: and I shall make all things well: and I will make all things well: and thou shalt see thyself that all manner of things shall be well." Where he saith "I may", I understand that the Father is meant: where he saith "I can", the Son: where he saith "I will", the Holy Ghost: where he saith "I shall", the unity of the blessed Trinity—three Persons and one Truth. And where he saith "thou shalt see thyself", I understand the oneing of all mankind that shall be saved into the blissful Trinity.

In these five words God sheweth his will that we should be enclosed in rest and in peace. Thus shall the ghostly thirst of Christ be ended. For this is the ghostly thirst of Christ—the love-longing that lasteth and ever shall, till we see that sight at doomsday. We that are to be safe, and to be Christ's joy and his bliss, some of us are still here, and others are yet to come; and some shall be here in that day. Therefore this is his thirst and his love-longing for us here: to gather us all in him unto our endless bliss (if I see it aright). For we are not yet as fully whole in him as we shall be then.

We know in our faith—and it was also shewed in all the Revelations—that Christ Jesus is both God and man. In respect of his Godhead he is himself highest bliss, and was so from without-beginning and so shall be without end—the self-same endless bliss, which can never be increased or diminished. This was plenteously seen in every shewing; and particularly in the twelfth, where he saith: "I it am that is Highest". In respect of his manhood (this too is known in our faith and was also shewed), Christ having the power of the Godhead suffered pains and passion and died, for love, in order to bring us to his bliss. These are the works of Christ's manhood wherein he hath his joy. This he shewed in the ninth Revelation, where he saith: "It is a joy, a bliss and an endless liking that ever I suffered passion for thee". This is the bliss of Christ in his works; and this is his meaning when he saith in the same shewing that we are his bliss, we are his prize, we are his worship, we are his crown.

In respect of his being our Head, Christ is glorified and impassible. But in respect of his body—in which all his members are knit—he is not yet fully glorified nor entirely impassible. The same thirst and longing that he had upon the rood-tree—that same desire, longing and thirst (if I see it aright) was in him from without-beginning; he hath the same now, and shall have, unto the time that the last soul to be saved shall have come up to his bliss. For as truly as there is in God the quality of ruth and pity, thus truly there is in God the quality of thirst and longing. And in virtue of this longing in Christ, we have to long, in our turn, for him; and without it no soul can come to heaven. This quality of longing and thirst cometh of the endless goodness of God, just as the quality of pity cometh of the same endless goodness (though, if I see it aright, longing and pity are separate qualities). In this goodness is the essence of the ghostly thirst, which is lasting in him as long as we are in need, drawing us up to his bliss. All this was seen in the shewing of his compassion; and that too shall cease at doomsday. Thus he hath ruth and compassion on us, and he hath longing to have us. But his wisdom and love permit not the end to come, until the best time.

THE THIRTY-SECOND CHAPTER

How all things shall be well and Scripture fulfilled; and we must steadfastly hold us in the faith of Holy Church, as is Christ's will

AT one time our good Lord said: "All things shall be well"; and at another he said: "Thou shalt see thyself that all manner thing shall be well". In these two sayings the soul received various manners of understanding. One was this: he willeth we know that he taketh heed not only of noble things and great, but also of little and small, low and simple—of both the one and the other. This is his meaning when he saith "all manner thing shall be well"; for he willeth we know that the least thing shall not be forgotten. Another understanding was this: there are many evil deeds done in our sight, and such great harm taken that it seemeth to us impossible that things should ever come to a good end. As we look upon these, we sorrow and mourn for them, so that we cannot rest in the blissful beholding of God—as we ought to do. The cause is that in the use of our reason we are now so blind, so lowly and so simple that we cannot know the high marvellous wisdom, the power and the goodness of the blissful Trinity. This is his meaning when he saith, "Thou shalt see thyself that all manner thing shall be well"; as if he said: "Accept it now faithfully and trustingly, and at the last end thou shalt see in truth and in fullness of joy".

So in the same five words beforesaid, "I may make all things well," I understand a mighty comfort in all the works of our Lord God that are to come. There is a deed which the blissful Trinity shall do in the last day (if I see it aright); but what that deed shall be, and how it shall be done, is unknown to all creatures which are beneath Christ, and shall be so until the time when it shall be done. The goodness and the love of our Lord God will us to know that it shall be done. But his might and wisdom by the same love will to hide and conceal from us what it shall be, and how it shall be done. The reason why he willeth us to know it just so, is because he willeth us to be easier in our souls and peaceable in loving, leaving aside the beholding of all troubles that could hinder our having true joy in him.

This is the great deed ordained by our Lord from without-beginning, treasured and hid in his blessed breast, known only to himself, by which he shall make all things well. For just as the blessed Trinity made all things from naught, right so the same blessed Trinity shall make all well that is not well.

In this sight I marvelled greatly and beheld our faith. I mean this: our faith is grounded in God's word; and it belongeth to our faith to believe that God's word shall stand in all points. One point of our faith is that many creatures shall be damned—for instance the angels who fell from heaven because of their pride, and are now fiends; and man on earth that dieth out of the faith of Holy Church, that is to say, those who are heathens; and also man that hath received christening but liveth an unchristian life and so dieth out of charity—all these shall be damned to hell without end, as Holy Church teacheth me to believe. In view of all this it seemed to me impossible that all manner of things should be well according as our Lord shewed in this time. But I had no other answer to the difficulty in this shewing of our Lord's, except this: "What is impossible to thee is not impossible to me; I shall save my word in all things—I shall make all things well."

Here I was taught by the grace of God that I should steadfastly keep me in the faith as I had understood it before, and that at the same time I should take my stand on and earnestly believe in what our Lord shewed in this time—that "all manner thing shall be well". For this is the great deed that our Lord shall do, in which he shall save his word in all things—he shall make well all that is not well. But what the deed shall be and how it shall be done there is no creature beneath Christ that knoweth it or shall know it until it is done—such was the understanding that I had of our Lord's meaning in this time.

THE THIRTY-THIRD CHAPTER

All damned souls are despised in the sight of God as the Devil is; and these Revelations do not take away the faith of Holy Church, but strengthen it; and the more we seek to know God's secrets, the less we know

AND yet in this I desired, as much as I durst, to have had some sight of hell and of purgatory—though it was not my meaning to put to the proof anything that belongeth to our faith. (For I believed firmly and truly that hell and purgatory have the same purpose that Holy Church teacheth them to have.) Rather my meaning was that I might have seen, for my instruction, in all things that belong to my faith, how I might live the more perfectly unto God's worship and my soul's progress. But for aught that I might desire I could see nothing at all of this, except (as is said before) in the fifth shewing, where I saw that the Devil is reproved by God and endlessly damned. By this sight I understood that of all creatures who are of the Devil's sort in this life and thus make their ending, there is no more mention made of them before God and his holy ones than there is of the Devil—notwithstanding that they are of man's kind, or whether they are christened or not.

For though the Revelation that was shewed was of goodness, and in it was made but little mention of evil, yet I was not drawn thereby from any point of faith that Holy Church teacheth me to believe. Hence, though in the sight I had of the passion of Christ in different shewings (in the first and the second, and in the fourth and the eighth wherein I had, in part, experience of the sorrow of our Lady and of the true friends of his that saw his pains—as it is before said), I did not see specified particularly the Jews that did him to death; yet notwithstanding this, I knew in my faith that they were accursed and damned without end, save those that were converted by grace. So was I strengthened and generally instructed to keep me in the faith, in each and every point, as I had understood it before: in the hope that I was therein by God's grace and mercy, and with the desire and prayer (such was my meaning) that I might continue therein unto my life's end.

It is God's will that we have great regard to all the deeds that he hath done. For he willeth by this regard that we know, trust and believe all that he shall do; but it evermore behoveth us to leave off considering what that deed shall be. So let us desire to be like our brethren the saints in heaven who have no will at all except God's will. Then only shall we have joy in God, and be well satisfied both with the hiding and the shewing. For in our Lord's meaning I saw truly that the more we busy ourselves about knowing his secrets in that or in any other thing, the farther off we shall be from the knowing.

THE THIRTY-FOURTH CHAPTER

God sheweth the secrets necessary to his lovers; and how they please God much who receive diligently the preaching of Holy Church

OUR Lord shewed two manners of secrets. One is this great secret with all the secret points that belong thereto. And these secrets he willeth we know as hid until the time that he will clearly shew them to us. The others are the secrets which he himself shewed openly in this Revelation. These are secrets which he willeth to make open and known to us; and he willeth us to know that it is his will for us to know them. They are secrets to us, not only because he wisheth them to be secrets to us, but on account of our blindness and our unknowing, for which he has great pity. Therefore he willeth to make them open to us himself, so that we may know him and love him, and cleave to him. For all that is expedient for us to wit and to know, with great courtesy our good Lord willeth to shew us what it is, along with all the preaching and teaching of Holy Church.

God shewed the very great pleasure that he taketh in all men and women who mightily and wisely receive the preaching and teaching of Holy Church. For he is Holy Church. He is its ground. He is its substance. He is its teaching. He is its teacher. He is the end and the reward towards which every kind soul travelleth. This is known, and shall be known to every soul to whom the Holy Ghost declareth it. And indeed I hope that all those who so seek shall speed; for they seek God. In the third shewing, then, where I saw that God does all that is done, I saw not sin; it was then I saw that all is well. But when God shewed me sin, then he said, "All shall be well".

THE THIRTY-FIFTH CHAPTER

How God doeth all that is good, and worshipfully permitteth, by his mercy, all that shall cease to be when sin is no longer permitted

AFTER God had shewed so plenteously and fully of his mercy, I desired to know concerning a certain creature that I loved, whether that creature would continue in the good life which I hoped was begun in the grace of God. By expressing this desire concerning an individual, it seemed that I hindered myself, because in that moment I received no teaching. Then I was answered in my reason as though by a friendly mediator: "Take what your Lord God shewed to you as spoken generally, beholding his courtesy. For it is greater worship to God to behold him in all things than in any particular thing." I consented, and there I learned that it is greater worship to God to know all things in general than to shew preference for any thing in particular. And if I would act wisely according to this teaching, I would not be moved to gladness by any one thing in particular, nor be greatly saddened by any thing at all. For "all shall be well"; and the fullness of joy is to behold God in all things.

For by the same blessed might, wisdom and goodness that he made all things, unto the same, as their end, our good Lord continually leadeth them, and himself shall bring them thereto. And when it is time, we shall see it. The reason of this was shewed in the first Revelation, and more clearly in the third, where it is said, "I saw God in a point".

All that our Lord doeth is rightful, and all that he suffereth is worshipful. In these two are comprehended good and evil. All that is good our Lord doeth, and all that is evil our Lord suffereth. I do not say that evil is worshipful, but I say that the sufferance of our Lord God is worshipful; for by it his goodness shall be known without end; and his meekness and mildness by his working of mercy and grace. Rightfulness is a thing so good that it cannot be better than it is. For God himself is very rightfulness, and all his works are done as rightfully as they are ordained from without-beginning, by his high might, his high wisdom and his high goodness—just as he hath ordained them for the best, even so he worketh continually, and leadeth them to the best end. He is ever fully pleased with himself and with all his works. The beholding of this blessed harmony is most sweet to the soul that seeth it by grace. All the souls that shall be saved are made rightful in heaven without end, in the sight of God, and by his own goodness. In this rightfulness we are endlessly kept and marvellously, above all creatures.

Mercy is a working that cometh of the goodness of God. And the working shall last as long as sin is permitted to pursue rightful souls. And when sin hath no longer leave to pursue, then the working of mercy shall cease. And then shall all be brought into rightfulness and stand therein without end. By his sufferance we fall; and in his blessed love, with his high might and wisdom, we are kept; and by mercy and grace we are raised to more manifold joy. Thus in rightfulness and in mercy he willeth to be known and loved now and without end. The soul that wisely beholdeth in grace, is well satisfied with both, and enjoyeth endlessly.

THE THIRTY-SIXTH CHAPTER

Of another excellent deed that our Lord shall do, which by grace may be known, in part, here; and how we should have joy in the same; and how God still doeth miracles

OUR Lord God shewed that a deed shall be done, and that he himself shall do it. It shall be worshipful and marvellous and plenteous; by him it shall be done, and he himself shall do it. And this is the highest joy that the soul understood—that God himself shall do it. Though I shall do right naught but sin, my sin shall not hinder his goodness working. I saw that the beholding of this is a heavenly joy in a God-fearing soul that evermore kindly, by grace, desireth God's will. This deed shall be begun here; it shall be worshipful to God and plenteously profitable to all his lovers on earth; and ever as we come to heaven we shall see it in marvellous joy. It shall last thus, in its working, until the last day; and the worship and the bliss of it shall last in heaven, before God and all his holy saints, without end. Thus was this deed seen, and understood in our Lord's meaning. And the reason why he shewed it is to make us have joy in him and in all his works.

When I saw that the shewing continued, I understood that there was meant a great thing that was to come—a thing (as God shewed) which he himself should do, and which hath the qualities before said. This he shewed most blissfully, meaning me to receive it wisely, faithfully and trustingly; but what the deed would be—that was kept a secret from me. In this I saw that it is not his will that we should fear to know the things he sheweth. He sheweth them because he willeth us to know them, and by the knowing he willeth us to love him and have liking in him and endlessly enjoy him. Because of the great love that he hath for us, he sheweth us all that is worshipful and profitable for the time. And even the things he willeth to keep hidden for now, of his great goodness he sheweth them as hid. And in this shewing his will is that we believe and understand that we shall see them truly in his endless bliss. Therefore it behoveth us to have our joy in him, for all that he sheweth and for all that he hideth. And if we willingly and meekly do so, we shall find therein great ease of mind and we shall have his endless thanks for it.

Here is the understanding of his words: "It shall be worshipful, marvellous and plenteous"—that is, to man in general or rather to all that shall be saved; "by me it shall be done, and God himself shall do it"—this shall be the highest joy that can be seen in this deed: that God himself shall do it, and man shall do right naught but sin. This then is our good Lord's meaning; it is as if he said:

Behold and see! Here hast thou matter for meekness, here hast thou matter for love, here hast thou matter for knowing thyself, here hast thou matter for joy in me. In this beyond all things thou canst please me most.

And as long as we are in this life, whenever in our folly we turn to behold the reproved, tenderly our Lord toucheth us and blissfully claspeth, saying in our soul: "Let be, my love, my most dear child, and attend to me (for I am enough to thee), and take joy in thy Saviour and thy salvation." That this is our Lord's working in us, I am sure; and the soul that is pierced within by grace shall see it and feel it. For though it is true that this deed must be taken as referring to man in general, yet it does not exclude the individual. What our good Lord willeth to do concerning his poor creatures is now unknown to me. But this deed and the afore-mentioned are not both the same, but two different ones. This one shall be known sooner; that is, as soon as we each come to heaven; and also it can be known here, in part, by those to whom our Lord giveth it. But the great deed afore-mentioned shall be known neither in heaven nor in earth until it be done.

Furthermore he gave me special understanding and teaching concerning the working and shewing of miracles, in this way: "It is known that I have worked miracles heretofore, many, most high, marvellous and worshipful and great. And as I have done, so I do now continually, and shall do in time to come." It is known that before miracles come sorrows and anguish and trouble. And the reason is that we might know our own feebleness and the mischief that we fall into by sin, and to make us meek and to make us cry to God for help and grace. Great miracles come after this, of the high might and wisdom and goodness of God—as he sheweth his power and the joys of heaven in as much as may be in this passing life, for the strengthening of our faith and increase of hope, in charity. Wherefore it pleaseth him to be known and worshipped in his miracles. His meaning then is that he willeth that we be not too overborne by the sorrows and tempestings that befall us. For it hath ever been so before coming of miracles.

THE THIRTY-SEVENTH CHAPTER

God keepeth his chosen full surely, although they sin; for in them is a godly will that never tasted sin

GOD brought to mind that I would sin. But because of the liking that I had in beholding him, I did not attend promptly to that shewing. But our Lord in his great mercy abode, and gave me the grace to attend. This shewing I took for myself, individually; but by all the gracious comfort that followed, as you shall see, I was taught to take it for all my evenchristians, in general and in no way individually. Here I conceived a gentle fear; but to it our Lord answered, "I keep thee full surely". This word was spoken with more love and assuredness of ghostly keeping than I can or may tell of. For just as it was first shewed to me that I would sin, for all my even-christians, right so was shewed the comfort, the sureness of keeping. (What could make me love more my evenchristians than to see in God that he loveth all that shall be saved as one soul, as it were?)

In every soul that shall be saved is a godly will that never assenteth to sin and never shall. Just as there is a beastly will in the lower part, which can will nothing good, so there is a godly will in the higher part—a will so good that it can never will evil but ever willeth the good. For this cause we are those whom he loveth, and endlessly we do what pleaseth him. This our good Lord shewed in the wholeness of love in which we stand together in his sight; so that he loveth us now, whilst we are here, as well as he shall do when we are there before his blessed face. And all our travail is for failing of love on our side.

THE THIRTY-EIGHTH CHAPTER

The sin of the chosen shall be turned to joy and worship; example of David, Peter and John of Beverley

GOD shewed that sin shall be no shame but rather worship for man. For right as for every sin, in truth, there is an answering pain, even so for every sin there is given a bliss to the same soul, by love. Right as different sins are punished by different pains, according to their grievousness, even so shall they be rewarded in heaven with different joys according as the sin has been painful and sorrowful to the soul on earth. The soul that shall come to heaven is so precious to God, and the place itself is so worshipful, that the goodness of God never permitteth a soul that is to come thither to sin finally. But what sinners they are that shall be so rewarded by overpassing worship is made known in Holy Church on earth, and also in heaven. For in this sight my understanding was lifted up into heaven, and God brought joyfully to my mind David, and with him others of the old law without number. And in the new law he brought to my mind first Magdalen, then Peter and Paul, Thomas and Jude, St John of Beverley and others also, without number; how that they are known in the Church on earth with their sins—that it is to them no shame, but all is turned to their worship. And our courteous Lord sheweth of them here in part, just as it is there in fullness, where the token of their sin is turned into worship.

And St John of Beverley—our Lord shewed him in his exaltation for our comfort and out of homeliness; he brought to my mind that he is a kind neighbour and of our knowing. And he called him St John of Beverley, just as we do; and that with a look most happy and sweet, shewing that St John is a very great saint in his sight, and a blissful one. At the same time he mentioned that in his youth and tender years he was God's most dear servant, most God-loving and God-fearing. And yet God permitted him to fall; but he kept him mercifully so that he did not perish nor lose any time. And afterwards God raised him to more manifold grace; for by the contrition and the meekness that he had in his living God hath given him in heaven manifold joys, far surpassing what he would have had if he had not sinned nor fallen. That this is true, God sheweth on earth by working plenteous miracles around his body constantly. All this shewing was to make us glad and merry.

THE THIRTY-NINTH CHAPTER

Of the sharpness of sin and the goodness of contrition; and how our kind Lord willeth us not to despair

SIN is the sharpest scourge that any chosen soul can be smitten with—a scourge which greatly afflicteth a man or woman, breaketh him in pieces and purgeth him of his self-love; to the extent that at times he thinketh himself fit for nothing but to sink into hell; until such time as, by the touching of the Holy Ghost, contrition overtaketh him and turneth his bitterness into hope in God's mercy. Then his wounds begin to heal and his soul to revive as he is converted to the life of Holy Church. The Holy Ghost leadeth him to confession to reveal his sins willingly, nakedly and truly; with great sorrow and with great shame for having so befouled the fair image of God. Then he undertaketh the penance for all his sins enjoined by his confessor, who is instructed in Holy Church by the teaching of the Holy Ghost. This is a meekness that greatly pleaseth God. He also meekly taketh bodily sickness that is of God's sending, and the sorrow and shame coming from without, of the reproof and despising of the world, with all manner of annoyance and temptation that may fall upon us, ghostly or bodily.

Most preciously our good Lord keepeth us when it seemeth to us that we are well nigh forsaken and cast away for our sins. And because we see that we have deserved it, and because of the meekness that we get thereby, we are raised high in God's sight, by his grace. Then also, when our Lord will, he visiteth us with his special grace, with such contrition and also with compassion and true longing to God that we are at once delivered of sins and pain, and lifted up to bliss, equal with the saints. By contrition we are made clean, by compassion we are made ready, by true longing for God we are made worthy. These are the three means, so I understood, whereby all souls come to heaven (that is to say, those that have been sinners) and shall be saved. It is by these medicines that every sinful soul must be healed. And after he is healed, his wounds are still seen before God—yet not as wounds but as honourable scars. Contrariwise, then, to our being punished here with sorrow and with penance, in heaven we shall be rewarded by the courteous love of our God almighty, who desireth that none that come thither should lose any degree of their labour. For he seeth sin as sorrow and pain to his lovers; and to them he assigneth no blame, for love.

The reward that we receive shall not be little; it shall be high, glorious and worshipful. And so shall all shame be turned into worship and joy. Our courteous Lord willeth not his servants to despair for often falling or for grievous falling. For our falling preventeth him not from loving us. Peace and love always exist and work in us, though we are not always in peace and in love. But he willeth that we take heed of this, that he is the ground of all our life in love; and furthermore that he is our everlasting Keeper, and mightily defendeth us against these enemies of ours who are full fell and full fierce upon us. (And our need is the greater the more we give them occasion, by our falling.)

THE FORTIETH CHAPTER

It behoveth us to long in love with Jesus, eschewing sin for love; the vileness of sin surpasseth all pains; and God loveth us well and tenderly whilst we are in sin; and so must we behave towards our neighbour

THIS is the sovereign friendship of our courteous Lord, that he keepeth us so tenderly whilst we are in our sins. And furthermore he toucheth us secretly and sheweth us our sins, by the sweet light of mercy and grace. But when we see ourselves so foul, then we think that God must be wroth with us for our sins; thus we are moved by the Holy Ghost, by his contrition, to pray and desire the amending of ourselves with all our might, so as to slake the wrath of God, until we find rest in soul and quiet of conscience. Then we hope that God hath forgiven us our sins. And truly he hath.

Then our courteous Lord sheweth himself to the soul cheerfully, with glad countenance, with a friendly welcome, as though the soul had been in pain and in prison, and speaketh so:

> My dear darling, I am glad thou art come to me; in all thy woe I have ever been with thee. And now thou seest me in my love, and we are oned in bliss.

Thus are sins forgiven by grace and mercy, and our soul worshipfully received in joy (just as it shall be when it comes to heaven), as often as we experience the grace-giving working of the Holy Ghost and the power of Christ's passion.

Here I fully understood that all manner of things are prepared for us by the great goodness of God; so that when at last we are ourselves in peace and in charity we shall be truly saved. But because we cannot have this in fullness whilst we are here, it is right for us ever to live in sweet praying and love-longing with our Lord Jesus; since he longeth ever to bring us to the fullness of joy—as was said before, when he shewed his ghostly thirst.

But if now, because of all this comfort that I have mentioned, any man or woman is foolishly tempted to say or to think that if this is true, it must be good to sin in order to have a greater reward, or else to attach less weight to sinning—let them beware of this temptation. For truly, if it come, it is false, and from the enemy. For the same true love that toucheth us all by his blessed strengthening, this same blessed love teacheth us to hate sin alone, for love. And I am certain by my own experience, that the more every kind soul seeth this, in the courteous love of our Lord, he is the more loth to sin; and the more is he ashamed of his sins. For if there were laid before us all the pains that are in hell and purgatory and earth, including death—all other pains than sin, we should choose all those pains rather than sin. Sin is so vile and so hateful that it cannot be likened to any pain that is not sin. And a kind soul hateth no pain other than sin; for all is good but sin, and nothing is evil but sin.

When we give our minds, by the working of mercy and grace, to love and meekness, we are made all fair and clean. As mighty and as wise as God is to save man, even so willing is he. For Christ himself is the ground of all the laws of

Christian men; he it is who taught us to do good and not evil. Here we may see that he is himself this Charity; and he doeth to us as he teacheth us to do to others. For he willeth that we be like him in wholeness of endless love to ourselves and to our even-christians. And as his love for us is never broken for our sins, even so it is his will that our love should not be broken either for ourselves or for our even-christians. But he willeth that we should hate the sin in itself, and endlessly love the soul of the sinner, as God loveth it; then we would hate sin as God hateth it, and love the soul as God loveth it.

These words, then, that God spoke "I keep thee most surely", are an endless comfort.

THE FORTY-FIRST CHAPTER

The fourteenth Revelation is as aforesaid; it is impossible that we should pray for mercy and lack it; and how God willeth us to pray always, though we be dry and barren, for that prayer is to him acceptable and pleasing

AFTER this, our Lord shewed me concerning prayer. In this shewing I saw two conditions for prayer—as our Lord understandeth it; one is rightfulness, the other is sure trust. For oftentimes our trust is not full; we are not sure that God heareth us, because (so we imagine) of our unworthiness, and the fact that we feel nothing at all—for we are as barren and as dry oftentimes after our prayers as we were before. Thus, in our feelings and in our folly is the cause of this weakness of ours; and this is my own experience.

All this our Lord brought to my mind at once, and shewed these words:

I am the ground of thy beseeching. First, it is my will

that thou have it—and seeing that I make thee to desire it, and seeing that I make thee to beseech it and thou beseechest it, how could it then be that thou shouldst not have thy beseeching?

Thus in the first reason, with the three that follow, our Lord shewed a mighty comfort, as may be seen in these same words. In the first reason, where he saith "and thou beseechest it", he there sheweth the exceeding pleasure and endless reward that he willeth to give us for our beseeching. And the sixth reason (where he says "How could it then be?") was given as an impossibility. For nothing is more impossible than that we should seek mercy and grace, and not have it. For all the things that our good Lord himself maketh us to beseech, these he hath ordained to us from withoutbeginning. Here then may we see that his proper goodness and not our beseeching is the cause of the goodness and the grace that he doeth to us; and that shewed he truly in all these sweet words where he saith "I am the ground". Our good Lord willeth that this be known amongst his lovers on earth; and the more we know it the more shall we beseech, if we understand it wisely—and that is our Lord's intention.

Beseeching is a true and grace-giving, lasting will of the soul which is oned and fastened to the will of our Lord, by the sweet and secret working of the Holy Ghost. Our Lord himself is the first receiver of our prayer—it is thus that I saw it; he receiveth it most thankfully and with great joy sendeth it up above and setteth it in the treasury, where it shall never perish. It is there before God and all his holy saints, received continually, ever speeding our needs. And when we come into our bliss, it shall be given us as a part of our joy, with his endless worshipful thanks.

Our Lord is full of mirth and gladness because of our prayer. For, with his grace, it maketh us as like to him in condition, as we are in kind; and such is his blessed will. He speaketh thus:

> Pray inwardly; though there seemeth to be no relish in it, yet it is profitable enough. Though thou shouldst feel naught, pray inwardly. Pray inwardly, though thou feelest naught, though thou seest naught, yea though it seemeth thou canst not pray for dryness and barrenness. In sickness and in feebleness thy prayer is full pleasant to me (though thou seemingly hast but little savour for it), and so is all thy living prayer in my sight.

Because of the reward and the endless thanks that he desireth to give us, he is covetous of having us pray continually in his sight. God accepteth the good will and the labour of his servants, no matter how we feel. Wherefore it pleaseth him that we should work in prayer and in good living by his help and his grace, reasonably and with discretion keeping our faculties turned towards him; until we have him whom we seek, in fullness of joy—that is, Jesus. And that shewed he in the fifteenth Revelation, where he saith, "Thou shalt have me for thy reward".

Also to prayer belongeth thanksgiving. Thanksgiving is a true inward knowing, a turning of ourselves with great reverence and loving dread and with all our power to the working which our Lord stirreth us to: inwardly, with joy and thanksgiving. And sometimes the abundance of it breaketh out into speech, and we say, "Good Lord, be merciful, blessed may thou be." And at other times when the heart is dry, and we feel nothing, or when tempted by our enemy, we are driven by reason and by grace to cry out loud on our Lord, rehearsing his blessed passion and his great goodness. And so the power of our Lord's word pierceth the soul and quickeneth the heart, and bringeth it by his grace into true working, maketh it to pray most blissfully and have true joy in our Lord. This is a most lovely thanksgiving in his sight.

THE FORTY-SECOND CHAPTER

Of three things that belong to prayer, and how we should pray; and of the goodness of God, that supplieth always for our imperfections and feebleness, when we do what we ought to do

Our Lord willeth us to have true understanding in what belongeth to our prayer, especially in three things. The first is to know by whom and how our prayer beginneth. By whom, he sheweth when he saith "I am the ground": and how, by his goodness; for he saith, "First, it is my will." The second is to know in what manner and how we should use our time of prayer; this is, that our will be turned to the will of our Lord in joy. This is his meaning when he saith "I make thee to will it". The third is to know the fruit and end of our prayer; which is to be oned and like to our Lord in everything. To this meaning and to this end was all this lovely lesson shewed. He will help us, and he shall bring it about, as he says himself, blessed may he be!

For this is our Lord's will—that our prayer and our trust be alike, large. For if we do not trust as much as we pray, we fail in full worship to our Lord in our prayer; and also we hinder and hurt ourselves. The reason is that we do not know truly that our Lord is the ground from whom our prayer springeth; nor do we know that it is given us by his grace and his love. If we knew this, it would make us trust to have of our Lord's gift all that we desire. For I am sure that no man asketh mercy and grace with sincerity, without mercy and grace being given to him first.

Sometimes it cometh to our mind that we have prayed

long time, and yet, seemingly, we have not received an answer. We should not be grieved on this account, but—and I am sure of this in our Lord's meaning—we merely await a better time, a greater grace, or a better gift. He willeth us to have true knowing in him—that he is all-being. In this knowing he willeth that our understanding be grounded, with all our power and all our intent and all our meaning. In this ground he willeth that we take up our station and our dwelling.

In his own grace-giving light he willeth that we have understanding of the three things that follow. The first is the nobility and the excellence of our creation; the second, our precious and most dear again-buying; the third, that everything beneath us he hath made to serve us, and preserveth it for our love. This then is his meaning; it is as if he said: "Behold and see that I have done all this before thy prayer; and now thou art, and prayest to me". He meaneth this also—that it is our part to know that the greatest deeds are done as Holy Church teacheth. And as we behold this with thanksgiving, we ought to pray for the deed that is now a-doing: that is, that he rule us and guide us in this life, to his worship, and bring us to his bliss. It is for this that he hath done everything. His meaning also is that we should see that he doeth it, and pray for it as well. But the latter is not enough; for if we pray and yet do not see that he doeth it, this maketh us heavy-hearted and full of doubt—which is not to his worship. And if we see that he doeth it, and yet pray not, we do not pay our debt. (And may that never be so!—which is to say, it is not so in his beholding.) But to see that he doeth it, and to pray forthwith—it is thus that he is worshipped and we sped.

All things that our Lord hath ordained, it is his will that we pray for them, either for particular things or for all in general. The joy and the bliss that he hath, and the thanks and the worship that we shall have, for this—it surpasseth the understanding of all creatures in this life, if I see it aright. For prayer is a right understanding of that fullness of joy that is to come, along with true longing and absolute trust that we shall savour and see the bliss that we are ordained to; which kindly maketh us to long. True understanding and love, with sweet grace-giving mindfulness in our Saviour, maketh us to trust; and thus it belongeth to our kind to have longing, and it belongeth to grace, to trust. In these two workings our Lord beholdeth us continually—for this is our duty, and his goodness cannot assign to us any lesser task than belongeth to our diligence to perform. And even when we do it, it shall seem to us as nothing. And true though this is, let us do what we can, and meekly ask for mercy and grace; and whatever is wanting in us, we shall find it in him. This is his meaning when he saith, "I am the ground of thy beseeching". In these blissful words and in the shewing I saw that all our wickedness and all our doubtful dreads may be fully overcome.

THE FORTY-THIRD CHAPTER

What prayer doeth when ordained to God's will; and how the goodness of God hath great liking in the deeds that he doeth concerning us—as though he were beholden to us, working all things most sweetly

PRAYER oneth the soul to God. For though the soul is ever like to God in kind, and like also in substance when restored by grace, it is often unlike to him in its condition, because of sin on man's part. But prayer is a witness that the soul willeth as God willeth, it strengtheneth a man's conscious working, and enableth him to receive grace. And hence he teacheth us to pray and mightily to trust that we shall have it. For he beholdeth us in love, and willeth to make us partakers of his good will and deed. Therefore he moveth us to pray for what it pleaseth him to do; and he willeth to reward us, and give us endless payment for the prayer and the good will that we have received of his gift. This was shewed in his words "and thou beseechest it". By these words God shewed such great pleasure and liking—as though he were beholden to us for every good deed that we do; and yet it is he that doeth it all. In as much, then, as we beseech him that we may do the thing that pleaseth him (it is as though he had said: "What couldst thou do to please me more than to beseech me mightily, wisely and willingly, that thou mayest do that which I will to have done?"); it is thus that the soul by its prayer is in accord with God.

But when our courteous Lord, of his special grace, sheweth himself to our soul, then we have what we desire; and we do not see, in that time, any thing more to pray for. All our intent and all our might is set wholly upon this beholding of him. And this is a high and ineffable prayer, as I see it. For all the reason why we pray is oned into the sight and the beholding of him to whom we pray, with marvellous enjoyment and reverent dread, and such great sweetness and delight in him that we can pray not at all, or only as he moveth us to do at the time. I know well that the more the soul seeth of God, the more she desireth him, by grace. But when we see him not so, then feel we need and cause to pray, because of our weakness and the unreadiness of ourselves to receive Jesus. For when a soul is tempested, troubled and left to herself because of her unrest, then it is time to pray, that she may make herself supple and docile, so as to receive God. (For by no manner of prayer can she make God supple to receive her: he is ever one and the same in his love.)

Thus I saw that whenever we see the need for prayer,

then our Lord is with us, helping our desire. But when, of his special grace, we behold him plainly and see no further need of prayer, then we are with him; for he draweth us to him by love. I saw and felt that his marvellous and super-abundant goodness filleth full all our powers; and saw also that his continual working in all manner of things is done so well, so wisely and so mightily that it surpasseth all our imagining—beyond all that we can explain or even conceive. Then we can do no more but behold him and enjoy: with a high and powerful desire to be entirely oned in him, to be received into his dwelling, to enjoy in his loving, to delight in his goodness. It is thus that we may, with his sweet grace in our own meek, continual prayer, come into him now, in this life, by many secret touchings and sweet ghostly sights and feelings, measured out to us according as our simpleness can support it. This is wrought, and shall be, by the grace of the Holy Ghost until we die in longing for love. Then shall we all come into our Lord—ourselves clearly knowing, God abundantly having—until we are all endlessly hid in God—him truly seeing and abundantly feeling, him ghostly hearing and delectably smelling, him all sweetly swallowing. And there shall we see God face to face. Homely and all-abundantly the creature that is made shall see and endlessly behold God who is the Maker. For no man may see God and live after, that is, in this mortal life. But when he will shew himself here, of his special grace, he strengtheneth the creature above the self, and measureth the shewing, according as this is his will and is profitable for the time.

THE FORTY-FOURTH CHAPTER

Of the properties of the Trinity; and how man's soul, a creature, hath the same properties in doing that which it was made for—seeing, beholding and marvelling at its God: so that, to itself, it seemeth as naught

GOD shewed, in all the Revelations, oftentimes, that man evermore worketh his will and his worship, lastingly and without stinting. What this working is, was shewn in the first Revelation, and that in a marvellous setting; for it was shewn in the working of the soul of our blissful Lady, Saint Mary, in her truth and wisdom. And how it was shewn, I hope, by the grace of the Holy Ghost, I shall tell as I saw.

Truth seeth God, and Wisdom beholdeth God; and of these two cometh the third; that is, a holy marvellous delight in God, which is love. Where truth and wisdom is verily there is love, which cometh of them both—and all of God's making. For God is endless sovereign Truth, endless sovereign Wisdom, endless sovereign Love, unmade; and man's soul is a creature in God, having the same properties, but made. Evermore it doeth that which it was made for—it seeth God, it beholdeth God, it loveth God. Wherefore God rejoiceth in the creature, the creature with endless marvelling, in God.

With marvelling the creature seeth his God, his Lord and his Maker, how he is so high, so great and so good in comparison with him that is made, that the creature seemeth as naught to himself. And yet the brightness and the clearness of truth and wisdom maketh him to see and to know that he is made for love; in which love God endlessly keepeth him.

THE FORTY-FIFTH CHAPTER

Of the firm deep judgement of God, and the variable judgement of man

GOD judgeth us upon our kind substance, which is ever kept whole and safe, one in him; and this judgement is of his righteousness. Man judgeth us upon our changeable sensuality, which seemeth, now one thing, now another, according as it is dominated by the parts, and sheweth outwards. Thus this judgement is variable: sometimes it is good and light, sometimes hard and heavy. In as much as it is good and light it belongeth to God's righteousness. But in as much as it is hard and heavy, our good Lord Jesus reformeth it by mercy and grace through the power of his blessed passion; and so he bringeth it into his righteousness. And though these two be thus accorded and oned, they shall be known separately in heaven, without end.

The first doom, which cometh of God's righteousness—that is, of his high endless life—is that fair sweet doom which was shewn throughout the fair Revelation, in which I saw him assign to us no kind of blame. And yet, though this was sweet and delightful in the beholding of it, I could not fully rest at ease, because of the judgement of Holy Church—as I had first understood it, and which was continually before my mind. For according to this judgement, methought I needs must acknowledge myself a sinner; and, by the same judgement, I understood that sinners are sometimes worthy of blame and wrath. But these two I could not see in God; and therefore my attention and desire were more than I can or may tell. For the higher judgement God himself shewed in this same time: hence I needs must accept it: whilst the lower judgement was taught me before this, in Holy Church: so that I might not, by any means, leave go the lower judgement.

This, then, was my desire: that I might see in God in what manner the judgement of Holy Church here on earth is true in his sight, and how it belongeth to me truly to acknowledge it; so that both judgements might be justified if this might be worshipful to God and the right way for me. To all this I had no other answer except a marvellous parable of a Lord and of a servant, as I shall say afterwards, and that full mistily shewn. Yet I stood in desire, and will so stand until my life's end, that I might understand by grace these two judgements, in so far as it belongeth to me to know. For all heavenly things and all earthly things that belong to heaven, are gathered up in these two judgements; and the more knowing and understanding, by the gracious leading of the Holy Ghost, that we have of these two judgements, the more we shall see and recognize our failings. And ever the more that we see them, the more naturally, by the help of grace, we shall long to be filled full of endless joy and bliss. For we are made thereto, and our substance is blessedly in God, and hath been after that it was made, and shall be without end.

THE FORTY-SIXTH CHAPTER

We cannot know ourselves in this life except by faith and grace; but we must acknowledge ourselves sinners. And how God is never wroth, being most near the soul, it keeping

THIS passing life that we lead here, in our sensuality, is not aware of what our true self is, except in faith. When we come to know and see truly and clearly what our self is, then shall we, truly and clearly, see and know our Lord God in fullness of joy. And therefore it needs must be that the nearer we are to our bliss, the more we shall long for it: and that both by nature and by grace. We can have knowing of our self in this life by the constant help and power of our high kind. In this knowledge we can increase and grow by the furthering and the speeding of mercy and grace; but we may never fully know our self up to our last moment—when this passing life, and all manner of woe and pain, shall have an end.

And therefore it properly belongeth to us, both by nature and by grace, to long and desire, with all our might, to know our self. For in this fullness of knowledge we shall truly and clearly know our God, in fullness of endless joy.

Yet in all this time, from beginning to end, I had two kinds of beholding. One was in endless and constant love, with sureness of his keeping and of my blissful safety. The other was in the ordinary teaching of Holy Church, in which I was, from the first, formed and grounded; which it was my will to have in use and in understanding. And the beholding of this never left me. For by the shewing I was never moved nor led therefrom in one single point; rather had I therein teaching to love it and like it; for in it I could, with the help of our Lord and his grace, have increase of and be lifted up to more heavenly knowing and higher loving.

In all this beholding, then, methought I must needs see and know that we are sinners and do many evil things that we ought to avoid; and leave many good deeds undone that we ought to perform. Wherefore we deserve pain and blame and wrath. Yet notwithstanding all this, I saw truly that our Lord was never wroth nor shall he ever be. For he is God: he is Good: he is Truth: he is Love: he is Peace. His Might, his Wisdom, his Charity and his Unity suffer him not to be wroth. For I saw truly that it is against the property of his Wisdom, and against the property of his Goodness. God is the goodness which may not be wroth; for God is naught but Goodness. Our soul is oned to him, the unchangeable Goodness; and between God and our soul is neither wrath nor forgiveness, in his sight. For our soul is so completely oned to God, through his own Goodness, that between God and our soul there can be nothing.

To the understanding of this was the soul led by love and drawn by might in every shewing. That it is thus, our good Lord shewed: and how it is thus, truly of his great goodness he will have us desire to learn: that is to say, in as much as it is proper for his creature to know it. For everything that this simple soul understood, God willeth should be shewn and known. But those things he will have secret, mightily and wisely he himself hideth, for love. For I saw in the same shewing that many a secret thing is hid, until the time that God of his goodness hath made us worthy to see it. Therewith I am well satisfied, abiding our Lord's will in these high marvels. And now I submit myself to my Mother, Holy Church, as a simple child should.

THE FORTY-SEVENTH CHAPTER

We must reverently marvel, and meekly yield ourselves, ever enjoying in God; and how our blindness, in that we see not God, is the cause of sin

ON two counts our soul must pay a debt; one is that we reverently marvel; the other is that we meekly endure, ever rejoicing in God. For he willeth us to know that in a short time we shall see clearly in him all that we desire. Notwithstanding all this, I beheld, and wondered greatly: "What is the mercy and forgiveness of God?" For by the teaching that I had before, I understood that the mercy of God means the forgiveness of his wrath, after the time that we have sinned. For methought that, to a soul whose intent and desire is to love, the wrath of God were harder than any other pain;

and therefore I took it that the forgiveness of his wrath should be one of the principal points of his mercy. But for aught that I might behold or desire to behold in all the shewings, I could not see this point.

But how I saw and understood the working of mercy, I shall say something of this, as God will give me grace. I understood it thus: man is changeable in this life: and through frailty and ignorance he falleth into sin. He is unmighty and unwise of himself: and also his will is overlaid whenever he is in tempest and in sorrow and woe. The cause of this is blindness: he seeth not God. For if he saw God continually, he would have no mischievous feeling nor any kind of stirring or sorrowing, which minister to sin. Such was my sight and experience at that time; and methought that the sight and the experience was high and plenteous and full of grace, concerning this our common feeling, in this life. Yet methought that it was but little and small compared with the great desire that the soul hath to see God.

Now I felt within me five affections working: they are: rejoicing, mourning, desire, dread and true hope. Rejoicing: for God gave me knowing and understanding that it was himself that I saw. Mourning: because of my failing. Desire: that I might see him ever more and more, yet understanding and knowing that we shall never have full rest until we see him clearly and truly, in heaven. Dread: for that it appeared, in all that time, that the sight should fail and I should be left to myself. True hope: because I saw that I should be kept in endless love by his mercy, and brought to his bliss.

The joy in this sight, with this true hope of his merciful keeping, made me to have feelings of comfort, so that the mourning and dread were not greatly painful. At the same time I beheld, in this shewing of God, that this kind of sight could not be continual in this life, both for the sake of his own worship, and for the increase of our endless joy. For this reason we fail oftentimes of the sight of him; and straightway we fall back into our self. Then find we this feeling—the contrariness which is in our self—springing from that old root of our first sin, along with all that cometh of our own furthering of it. And in this we are travailed and tempted with the feeling of sin and of pain in many diverse ways, ghostly and bodily; such is our experience in this life.

THE FORTY-EIGHTH CHAPTER

Of mercy and grace; and their properties; and how we shall rejoice that ever we suffered woe patiently

OUR good Lord the Holy Ghost, who is endless life dwelling in our soul full truly, keepeth it and worketh therein a peace, and bringeth it to ease by grace, and maketh it docile to God, and in accord with him. This is the way of mercy in which our good Lord continually leadeth us as long as we are in this changeable life. For I saw no wrath except on man's part: and that forgiveth he in us.

Wrath is naught else but a frowardness and a contrariness to peace and love, which cometh of failing of might, or of wisdom, or of goodness; which failing is not in God, but on our part. For we, by sin and wretchedness, have in us a wrath and a continual contrariness to peace and to love. This shewed he full often in his lovely look of ruth and pity. For the ground of mercy is in love: and the working of mercy is our being kept in love.

This was shewed in such a manner that I was unable to perceive of the property of mercy except as it were all love, in love. I mean, this is what I saw: Mercy is a sweet gracious working, in love, mingled with plenteous pity. Mercy worketh in the keeping of us. Mercy worketh in turning all things to good in us. Mercy, for love, suffereth us to fail in a measure. In as much as we fail, in so much we fall; and in as much as we fall, in so much we die. For we must needs die in as much as we fail of the sight and the awareness of God who is our life. Our failing is dreadful, our falling is shameful, and our dying is sorrowful.

But yet in all this the sweet eye of pity and of love departeth never from us, and the working of mercy ceaseth not. For I beheld the property of mercy, and I beheld the property of grace—two ways of working in the one love. Mercy is a property full of pity; it belongeth to the Motherhood of tender love. Grace is a worshipful property; it belongeth to the royal Lordship of the same love. Mercy worketh by preserving, permitting, quickening and healing: and all in tenderness of love. Grace worketh with mercy, by lifting up, rewarding, endlessly surpassing all that our loving and our travail deserveth, spreading abroad and making plain the high abundance and largesse of God's royal Lordship in his marvellous courtesy. All this cometh of the abundance of love. For grace worketh our dreadful failing into plenteous and endless solace. Grace worketh our shameful falling into high worshipful rising. Grace worketh our sorrowful dying into holy blessed life.

For I saw full truly that ever as our contrariness worketh unto us, here on earth, pain, shame and sorrow: right so, and contrariwise, grace worketh unto us, in heaven, solace, worship, bliss, to overflowing; so far forth, that when we shall go up and receive that sweet reward which grace hath wrought, there we shall thank and bless our Lord endlessly, rejoicing that ever we suffered woe. This property of blessed love we shall know in God, which we might never have known, had not woe gone before. When I saw all this, I needs must grant that the mercy of God and the forgiveness slaketh and wasteth our wrath.

THE FORTY-NINTH CHAPTER

Our life is grounded in love; without the which we perish. God is never wroth, but in our wrath and sin, he mercifully keepeth us, and regarding our tribulations, treateth with us unto peace

HERE was a high marvel, shewn continually in all the Revelations to the soul, and beheld with great diligence; that our Lord, in himself, may not forgive because he may not be wroth; it were impossible. This was shewed: that our life is all grounded and rooted in love. Hence to the soul that seeth so far forth into the high marvellous goodness of God as to see that we are endlessly oned to him in love, nothing could be more impossible than that God should be wroth. For wrath and friendship are two contraries. He that layeth and destroyeth our wrath, and maketh us meek and mild—we must needs believe that he is ever, in the same love, meek and mild; which is contrary to wrath.

For I saw full truly that where our Lord appeareth, peace is established and wrath hath no place. I saw no manner of wrath in God, neither for a short time, nor for long. For truly, as I see it, if God could be wroth a while, we should have neither life, nor place, nor being. As truly as we have our being of the endless might of God, and of the endless wisdom, and of endless goodness; so also we have our keeping in the endless might of God, in the endless wisdom, and in the endless goodness. For though we feel in our self wrath, conflict and strife, yet we are all mercifully beclosed in the mildness of God and in his meekness, in his benignity and in his kindliness.

I saw full truly that all our endless friendship, our station, our life and our being, is in God. The same endless goodness which keepeth us, when we sin, so that we perish not, that same endless goodness continually treateth with us unto a peace, against our wrath and our contrarious falling. It maketh us to see our need, and, with a true dread, mightily to seek unto God to have forgiveness, with a gracious desire of our salvation. For we cannot be blessedly saved until we be truly in peace and in love: which itself is our salvation. And though, by the wrath and the contrariness that is in us, we are now in tribulation, distress and woe through falling into blindness and helplessness, yet are we sure and safe by the merciful keeping of God which preventeth our perishing.

Yet we shall not be blessedly secure in the possession of our endless joy, until we be wholly in peace and in love: that is to say, full pleased with God, and with all his works and with all his judgements; and loving and at peace with our self, and with our even-christian, and with all that God loveth; as Love liketh. This is what God's goodness doeth in us. Thus I saw that God is our very peace, and our sure Keeper when we be, ourselves, at unpeace. He continually worketh to bring us unto endless peace.

And when, by the working of mercy and grace, we are made meek and mild, then are we full safe; suddenly is the soul oned to God, when it is truly peaced in the self: for in him is found no wrath. Thus I saw that when we are wholly in peace and in love, we find no contrariness, no manner of hindering. Whilst the contrariness which is now in us—our Lord God, of his goodness, maketh it to us full profitable. For though contrariness is the cause of all our tribulation and all our woe, our Lord Jesus taketh these and sendeth them up to heaven; where they are made more sweet and delectable than heart may think or tongue can tell. And when we come thither we shall find them, already turned into true fairness and endless worship. God, then, is our steadfast ground, and shall be our full bliss; he shall make us unchangeable even as he is, when we shall be there.

THE FIFTIETH CHAPTER

How the chosen soul was never dead in the sight of God: and of a marvel concerning the same. How three things emboldened her to ask of God the understanding of this

IN this mortal life mercy and forgiveness is our way, that ever more leadeth us to grace. Through the tempest and the sorrow that we fall into, on our side, we be often dead—according to man's judgement on earth. But in the sight of God, the soul that shall be safe was never dead nor shall ever be. Yet in this I wondered and pondered with all the diligence of my soul, after this fashion: "Good Lord, I see thee—that thou art very truth; and I know truly that we sin grievously all day, and are most blameworthy. I cannot evade the knowing of this truth, yet I see not thee shewing to us any manner of blame. How may this be?" I knew by the common teaching of Holy Church, and by my own consciousness, that the blame of our sins continually hangeth upon us, from the first sin unto the time that we come up into heaven. Herein was my wonderment—that I saw our Lord God shewing to us no more blame than if we were as clean and holy as the angels are in heaven. Between these two opposites my reason was greatly travailed, because of my blindness, and could find no rest for fear that his blessed presence should pass from my sight, and I be left in unknowing as to how he beholdeth us in our sin. For either I must needs see in God that sin were all done away; or else I must needs see in God how he seeth it, whereby I might truly know how it belongeth to me to see sin, and the manner of our blame. My longing endured, in my continual beholding of him; yet I could have no patience in my great fear and perplexity, whilst I thought: "If I take it thus, that we are not sinners nor blameworthy, then it seemeth as though I should err in failing to acknowledge the truth. But granted this truth—that we are sinners and blameworthy, good Lord, how may it then be that I cannot see this truth in thee, who art my God and my Maker: in whom I desire to see all truth? Three reasons make me bold to ask this question. The first is that it is so low a thing—for if it were an high, I should be afraid to ask it. The second is that it is so common a thing—for if it were special and secret, also I should be afraid to ask it. The third is that I need to know, as it seemeth to me, if I am to go on living here, for the knowing of good and evil: how I may, by reason and by grace, part them asunder, and love goodness and hate evil, as Holy Church teacheth." So I cried, inwardly, with all my might, seeking unto God for help, on this fashion: "O Lord Jesus, King of bliss, how shall I find ease? Who shall tell me and teach me what it needeth me to know, if I cannot, at this time, see it in thee?"

THE FIFTY-FIRST CHAPTER

The answer to the doubt aforesaid, by a marvellous parable of a lord and a servant; and God willeth that we abide his coming—for it was nearly twenty years after, ere she fully understood this parable. How it is to be understood that Christ sitteth on the right hand of the Father

THEN our courteous Lord answered in shewing full mistily a wonderful parable of a lord that hath a servant; and gave me a sight for the understanding of both. This sight was shewed double in regard of the lord; and it was shewed double in regard of the servant. The first part was shewed ghostly in bodily likeness; the second part was shewed more ghostly without bodily likeness. As for the first part, I saw thus: two persons in bodily likeness—that is to say, a lord and a servant. And with this sight God gave me ghostly understanding: the lord sitteth in solemn state, in rest and in peace. The servant standeth before his lord reverently, ready to do his lord's will. The lord turneth upon his servant a look full of love, sweet and meek. He sendeth him into a certain place, to do his will. The servant not only goeth, but starteth out suddenly, and runneth in great haste, for love, to do his lord's will. But straightway he falleth down into a ravine, and taketh full great hurt; and then he groaneth and moaneth, waileth and turneth about, but he cannot rise or help himself in any manner. In all this, the most misfortune that I saw him in was failing of comfort; for he could not turn his face to look upon his loving lord, in whom is full comfort; though he was very close to him. But, as a man that was full feeble and unwise for the time, he attended only to his lasting feeling of woe. In this he suffered seven great pains. The first was the sore bruising that he had taken in his fall, which was to him great pain. The second was the heaviness of his body. The third was the feebleness following on these two. The fourth was that he was blinded in his reason and stunned in his mind; so much so that he had almost forgotten all care for himself. The fifth was that he could not rise. The sixth pain was to me the most marvellous, and this was that he lay all alone. I looked all about and beheld: but far or near, high or low, I saw no help for him. The seventh was that the place which he lay in was lonely, hard and grievous. I marvelled how this servant could thus meekly suffer all this woe. And I beheld with deliberation to discover if I could perceive in him any fault; or whether the lord would assign to him any kind of blame. And truly there was none seen; for his good will and his great desire were the only cause of his falling. He was as lovable and as good inwardly as he was when he stood before his lord, ready to do his will. Right thus, continually, his loving lord full tenderly beholdeth him; and now with a double regarding; one outward, full meekly and mildly, with great ruth and pity—and this was seen in the first shewing; another inward, more ghostly, which was shewed with a leading of my understanding into the Lord. In this sight I saw him highly rejoicing for the worshipful rest and the high honour that he will, and shall, bring his servant to by his plenteous grace. And this was part of that second shewing. Then was my understanding led again into the first shewing—both remaining in my mind; it was as though the courteous lord said: "Lo, my beloved servant! What harm and evil he hath had and endured in my service, for love of me, yea, and because of his good will! Is it not right that I should reward him, considering his fear and his dread, his hurt and his maiming, and all his woe? And besides all this, falleth it not to me to give him a gift that is better and more worshipful to him than his own wholeness should have been? Else, me thinketh I would give him no thanks." Here an inward ghostly shewing of the Lord's meaning descended into my soul; in which I saw that it must needs be in accord with his great goodness and his own worship that his very dear servant, whom he loved so much, should be highly and blissfully rewarded without end; above what he should have been if he had not fallen. Yea, and so far forth that his falling, and all the woe that he hath suffered thereby, shall be turned into high over-passing worship, and endless bliss. At this point the shewing of the parable vanished: and our good Lord led forth my understanding unto sight and shewing of the Revelation, to the end. But notwithstanding all this forthleading, my wonderment at the parable never went from me. For methought that it was given to me as an answer to my desire; and yet I could not have therein full understanding unto peace of mind, in that time. For in the servant (who, as I shall say, was shewed for Adam) I saw many diverse properties that could in no way be ascribed to the single Adam. And thus, in that time, I took my stand especially on three knowings, for the full understanding of this marvellous parable was not given me at that time. In this dark parable the secrets of the whole Revelation were yet much hid. (But this notwithstanding, I saw and understood that every shewing is full of secrets.) Now, therefore, I must tell of these three properties in which I have found some relief. The first is the beginning of teaching which I understood therein, at the time. The second is the inward learning I have received therein since then. The third is the whole Revelation from beginning to end, which our Lord God of his goodness bringeth often and liberally to the sight of my understanding. These three are so oned in my understanding of them that I cannot nor may not separate them; and by these three, as one, I have teaching whereby I ought to believe and trust in our Lord God, that of the same goodness whereof he shewed it, and for the same end: right so, of the same goodness and for the same end, he shall make it clear to us when it shall be his will. Twenty years after the time of the shewing, save three months, I had teaching inwardly, as I shall say: "It belongeth to thee to take heed of all the properties and conditions that were shewed in the parable, though it seemeth that this be misty and unyielding to thy regarding." I assented willingly and with great desire; examining inwardly and with deliberation all the points and properties that were shewed, in that same time, as far forth as my wits and my understanding would serve me, beginning at the lord and the servant: the manner of the sitting of the lord, and the place he sat on; the colour of his clothing; his form; his outward appearance and nobility; his inward goodness; the manner of the servant's standing, and the place; its where and how; the manner of his clothing, its colour and form; his outward behaviour, and his inward goodness—his attractiveness. The lord that sat in solemn state, in rest and in peace, I understood that he is God. The servant that stood before him, I understood that he was shewed for Adam: that is to say, one man was shewed, in the time of his falling, to make thereby to be understood how God beholdeth every man and his falling. For in the sight of God every man is one man, and one man is every-man. This man was hurt in his powers, and made full feeble; and he was stunned in his understanding, in that he was turned from the beholding of his Lord. But his will was preserved in God's sight; for his will I saw our Lord commend and approve. But he himself was hindered and blinded in the knowing of this true will; which is the cause to him of great sorrow and grievous distress. For he neither seeth clearly his loving Lord, who is full meek and mild towards him; nor seeth he truly how he himself is in the sight of his loving Lord. And well I wot, when these two be wisely and truly seen, we shall get rest and peace, in part here, and their fullness in bliss, in heaven: by his plenteous grace.

This was a beginning of teaching which I saw in the same time: whereby I might come to know in what manner he beholdeth us in our sin. Next I saw that only pain blameth and punisheth: but our courteous Lord comforteth and succoureth. Ever he is of glad countenance to the soul, loving us, and longing to bring us to his bliss.

The place that the Lord sat on was unadorned—the earth, a barren desert, a solitary wilderness. His clothing was ample and flowing, full seemly as befitteth a Lord. The colour of it was blue as the sky, fair but not gaudy. His mien was merciful; and the colour of his face was a fair brown-white, the features well-proportioned: his eyes were dark and very beautiful, full of a lovely pity; and within him a high world, long and broad, all full of endless heavenliness. The loving look that he turned upon his servant continually and especially in his falling—methought it might melt our hearts for love, and break them in two for joy. This fair looking shewed itself as a seemly mingling which was marvellous to behold. One part was ruth and pity, the other joy and bliss. The joy and bliss overpass the ruth and pity as far as heaven is above earth; the pity was earthly, and the bliss heavenly. The ruth and pity of the Father was for the falling of Adam, who is his most beloved creature. The joy and the bliss was for the falling of his most dear Son, who is equal with the Father. The merciful beholding of his lovely face filled full all the earth, and descended down with Adam unto hell; and by this continual pity Adam was kept from endless death. This mercy and pity dwell with mankind unto the time that we come up into heaven. But man is blinded in this life; and therefore we may not see our Father, God, as he is. But what time he, of his goodness, will shew himself to man, he sheweth himself in homely fashion, as man. Notwithstanding that sight, I saw verily that we ought to know and believe that the Father is not man; rather, this sitting on the earth, barren and desert, must be taken to mean that he made man's soul to be his own city and his dwelling place; which is most pleasing to him of all his works. But what time man was fallen into sorrow and pain, he was not in fit state to fulfil that noble office. Therefore our gracious Father would prepare himself no other place, but would sit upon the earth abiding mankind—which is mingled with earth—till what time, by his grace, his well-beloved Son had brought back his city into its noble fairness, with his hard travail.

The blueness of the clothing betokeneth his steadfastness; the brown colour of his fair face, with the lovely dark hue of the eyes, was most fit to shew his holy seriousness of purpose. The ample nature of his clothing which was shining fair about him, betokeneth that in him are enclosed all heavens and all endless joy and bliss. All this was shewed in a moment, where I say that "mine understanding was led into the Lord". In this moment, I saw him highly rejoice for the worshipful restoring that he will and shall bring his servant to, by his plenteous grace.

And still I marvelled, beholding the Lord and the servant aforesaid. I saw the Lord sitting solemnly; and the servant standing reverently before his Lord. In this servant there is a double understanding: one outward, the other inward. Outwardly, he was clad simply, as a labourer who is ready for his work. He stood very near to the Lord, not straight in front of him, but a little to one side—on the left. His clothing was a white kirtle, single, old, and all bestained; dyed with the sweat of his body, close-fitting and short, about a hand's breadth below the knee, threadbare, as though it would soon be worn out, ready to be ragged and rent. And in this I marvelled greatly, thinking: "Now this is unseemly clothing for the servant that is so highly bred to stand in, before so worshipful a Lord!" But inwardly, in him was shewed a ground of love—the love which he had to the Lord; it was equal to the love which the Lord had to him. The servant, of his wisdom, saw inwardly that there was but one thing to do that should be to the worship of the Lord. And the servant, for love, having no regard to himself nor to anything that might befall him, hastily did start and run, at the sending of his Lord, to do that which was his will and his worship. It seemed, by his outward clothing, as though he had been in continual labour, and a hard worker for a long time. But by the inward sight that I had, both of the Lord and of the servant, it seemed that he was a new servant: that is to say, now beginning his work—a servant who was never sent out before.

There was a treasure in the earth, which the Lord loved. I marvelled and thought what it might be. And I was answered in my understanding: "It is a food which is lovesome and pleasant to the Lord." For I saw the Lord sit, as a man, and I saw neither food nor drink wherewith to serve him. This was one marvel. Another marvel was that this worthy Lord had no servant but one, and him he sent out. I beheld, thinking what manner of labour it might be that the servant would do. And then I understood that he would do the greatest labour and the hardest travail that there is: he would be a gardener, delving and dyking and sweating, and turning the earth up and down: he would seek the depths, and water the plants in season; and in this he would continue his travail, and make sweet floods to run, and noble plenteous fruit to spring forth. This fruit he would bring before the Lord, and serve him therewith to his liking; he would never return until he had made this food all ready, as he knew it would please his Lord; then he would take this food, with the drink, and bear it full worshipfully before the Lord. And all this time the Lord would sit, right in the same place, abiding the servant whom he sent out. Still I marvelled whence the servant came. For I saw in the Lord that he hath within himself endless life and all manner of goodness, save the treasure that was in the earth. And that, too, was grounded in the Lord, in marvellous deepness of endless love; but it was not all to his worship until his servant should have thus nobly prepared it, and brought it before him, presenting it in himself. Outside the Lord was right naught but wilderness.

I understood not all what this parable meant; and therefore I marvelled whence the servant came.

In the servant is comprehended the second person of the Trinity. And in the servant is comprehended Adam: that is to say, every-man. Thus, when I say "the son", this meaneth the Godhead which is equal to the Father's; and when I say "the servant", it meaneth Christ's manhood which is the true Adam. By the nearness of the servant is understood the Son; and by the standing at the left side is understood Adam.

The Lord is God the Father: the servant is the Son Jesus Christ. The Holy Ghost is the equal love which is in them both. When Adam fell, God's son fell; because of the true oneing which was made in heaven, God's Son could not be separated from Adam. (By Adam I understand every-man.) Adam fell from life to death unto the deeps of this wretched world, and after that into hell. God's Son fell, with Adam, into the deeps of the Maiden's womb, who was the fairest daughter of Adam; and that, for to excuse Adam from blame in heaven and earth; and mightily he fetched him out of hell. By the wisdom and the goodness that was in the servant is understood God's Son; by the poor clothing of the labourer, standing near the left side, is understood the manhood of Adam, with all the mischief and feebleness that followeth. For in all this our good Lord shewed his own Son and Adam as one man. The power and the goodness that we have is of Jesus Christ; the feebleness and blindness that we have is of Adam: which two were shewed in the servant. Thus hath our good Lord Jesus taken upon him all our blame. And therefore our Father nor may nor will any more blame assign to us than to his own well-beloved Son Jesus Christ. Thus was he the servant, before his coming into earth, standing ready before the Father in purpose, till what time he would send him to do the worshipful deed by which mankind was brought again into heaven. That is to say: notwithstanding that he is God, equal with the Father in respect of the Godhead; in his foreseeing purpose he would be man, to save man, in the fulfilling of the will of his Father.

So he stood before his Father as a servant, willingly taking upon himself all our charge. Then he set forth, full readily, at the Father's will. And straightway he fell, full low into the Maiden's womb; having no regard to himself, nor to his hard lot. The white kirtle is his flesh; its singleness, that there was right naught between the Godhead and the manhood; its straitness is poverty; its age of Adam's wearing; its stains, the sweat of Adam's travailing; its shortness sheweth the servant as labourer. And thus I saw the servant, as it were saying: "Lo, my dear Father, I stand before thee in Adam's kirtle, all ready to set out, and to run. I would be on the earth, to thy worship, whenever it is thy will to send me. How long must I desire it?" Full truly the Son knew when it would be the Father's will, and how long he must desire—that is to say, in respect of the Godhead; for he is the Wisdom of the Father. Wherefore this saying was shewed in the understanding of the manhood of Christ. For all mankind that shall be saved by the sweet incarnation and the passion of Christ, all is the manhood of Christ. He is the head and we are his members. To the members, the day and the time is unknown, when every passing woe and sorrow shall have an end, and the everlasting joy and bliss shall be fulfilled. To see this day and time, all the company of heaven longeth or desireth. And all those under heaven who shall come thither—their way is by longing and desiring; which longing and desiring was shewed in the servant's standing before the Lord; or else in the Son's standing before the Father in Adam's kirtle. For the longing and desiring of all mankind that shall be saved appeared in Jesus. Jesus is all that shall be saved, and all that shall be saved is Jesus; and all this of the charity of God, with the obedience, meekness and patience, and the virtues that belong to us.

Further, in this marvellous parable, I have teaching within me, as it were the beginning of an ABC, whereby I may have some understanding of our Lord's meaning. For all the privities of the whole Revelation are hid therein; notwithstanding that all the shewings are full of privities. The sitting of the Father betokeneth the Godhead; that is to say, it sheweth rest and peace; for in the Godhead there can be no travail. And that he sheweth himself as Lord betokeneth our manhood. The standing of the servant betokeneth travail; on the left side, that he was not full worthy to stand straight in front of the Lord. His starting was the Godhead, and the running was the manhood. For the Godhead starteth from the Father, into the Maiden's womb: falling down into the taking of our nature. And in this falling he took great sore. The sore that he took was our flesh; in which, from the first, he had experience of mortal pains. The fact that he stood in awe before the Lord, and not straight in front of him, betokeneth that his clothing was not suited to the standing straight in front of the Lord; that could not, nor should not be his place as long as he was a labourer. Nor might he sit with the Lord in rest and peace till he had won his peace, rightfully, with his hard travail. And by the left side is meant that the Father allowed his own Son, willingly, in the manhood, to suffer all man's pain, without sparing him. That his kirtle should be almost in rags and tatters is understood to mean the rods and scourges, the thorns and the nails, the drawing and the dragging, his tender flesh rending (as I saw in some measure: the flesh was torn from the skull, hanging in little pieces, until the bleeding stopped, and it began to dry and cling again to the bone). And by the wallowing and the writhing, the groaning and mourning, is understood that he could never rise again almightily (from the time that he was fallen into the Maiden's womb), until his body was slain and dead, and he yielded his soul into the Father's hand along with all mankind for whom he was sent. At this point he began first to shew his might. For then he went into hell; and when he was there, then he raised up the great host out of the deep abyss, which had been truly knit to him in high heaven. His body lay in the grave until Easter morrow; but from that time he lay never more. For there was truly and rightly ended the wallowing and the writhing, the groaning and the mourning. Our foul mortal flesh that God's

Son took upon himself, which was Adam's old kirtle, strait, threadbare and short, then by our Saviour was made fair, new, white and bright, of endless cleanness, large and ample: fairer and richer than was the clothing which I saw on the Father. For that clothing was blue; but Christ's clothing is now of a fair, seemly blending of colours which is so marvellous that I cannot describe it: for it is all of very worship. Now sitteth not the Lord on the earth in the wilderness; but he sitteth on his rich and noble seat which he made in heaven, most to his liking. Now standeth not the Son before the Father, as a servant before the Lord in awe, and half-naked; but he standeth before the Father on an equality, richly clothed in blissful fullness, with a crown upon his head of precious richness. For it was shewed that we are his crown—the crown which is the Father's joy, the Son's worship, the Holy Ghost's liking, and endless marvellous bliss to all that are in heaven. Now standeth not the Son before the Father on the left side, as a labourer; but he sitteth on the Father's right hand in endless rest and peace. (By this is not meant that the Son sitteth on the right hand beside his Father, as one man sitteth by another, in this life. For there is no such sitting, as I understand it, in the Trinity. But he sitteth on the Father's right hand: that is to say, right in the highest nobility of the Father's joy.)

Now is the spouse, God's Son, in peace, with his beloved wife, who is the fair maiden of endless joy. Now sitteth the Son, very God and very man, in his city in rest and in peace: the city which his Father hath allotted to him in his endless purpose; and the Father in the Son, and the Holy Ghost in the Father and in the Son.

THE FIFTY-SECOND CHAPTER

God rejoiceth that he is our Father, Brother and Spouse. How the Chosen have here a mingling of weal and woe: but God is with us in three ways. And how we may eschew sin: but never perfectly, as in heaven

AND then I saw that God rejoiceth that he is our Father: and God rejoiceth that he is our Mother: and God rejoiceth that he is our true Spouse, and our soul his beloved wife. And Christ rejoiceth that he is our Brother: and Jesus rejoiceth that he is our Saviour.

These are five high joys, as I understand, in which he willeth that we rejoice, him praising, him thanking, him loving, him endlessly blessing—all those that shall be saved. During the time of this life, we have in us a marvellous mingling both of weal and of woe. We have in us our Lord Jesus Christ, uprisen; and we have in us the wretchedness and mischief of Adam's falling. Dying, by Christ we are steadfastly kept; and by touching of his grace, we are raised into sure trust of salvation. But by Adam's falling, we are so broken in our feelings, in various ways, by sins and by sundry pains, in which we are made dark and so blind that we can find scarcely any comfort. But in our intentions we abide God, and faithfully trust to have mercy and grace; and this is his own working in us. He, of his goodness, openeth the eye of our understanding: by which we have sight: sometimes more and sometimes less, according as God giveth us the ability to receive it. At one time we are lifted up into the first, at another we are suffered to fall into the other. Thus this mingling is so perplexing in us, that we scarcely know, either concerning ourselves, or our fellow-christians in what way we stand; such is the marvellous nature of these various feelings. But yet, in each holy assent that we give to

God when we experience him truly, willing to be with him with all our heart and with all our soul and with all our might, then indeed we hate and despise our evil stirrings, and all that might be an occasion of sin, ghostly or bodily. But again, when this sweetness is hid, we fall again into blindness, and so into woe and tribulation, in various ways; and then this is our comfort—that we know in our faith that by the power of Christ who is our Keeper, we assent never thereto. Rather we strive there against, and endure, in pain and in woe: praying, unto the time that he sheweth himself again to us. Thus we stand in this mingling all the days of our life. But it is his will that we trust that he is lastingly with us; and this in three ways. He is with us in heaven, true man, us updrawing into his own person; this was shewed in the ghostly thirst. He is with us on earth, us leading; this was shewed in the third Revelation, where I saw God in a point. And he is with us in our soul, endlessly dwelling, ruling and guiding us; this was shewed in the sixteenth Revelation, as I shall say.

In the servant, then, was shewed the blindness and the mischief of Adam's falling; and in the servant was shewed the wisdom and goodness of God's Son. In the Lord was shewed the ruth and pity for Adam's woe; and in the Lord was shewed the high nobility and endless worship that mankind is come to by the power of the passion and the death of his well-beloved Son. Wherefore he mightily rejoiceth in his falling, for the high raising and fullness of bliss that mankind is come into, overpassing what we should have had, if he had not fallen. It was to see this overpassing nobility that my understanding was led unto God, in the same time that I saw the servant fall. So we have now matter for mourning, because our sin is the cause of Christ's pains; and we have, lastingly, matter for joy, because endless love made him to suffer. And therefore the creature that seeth and feeleth the working of love, by grace, hateth naught except sin. (Of all things, in my sight, love and hate are the hardest and most immeasurable contraries.)

But notwithstanding all this, I saw and understood in our Lord's meaning, that we cannot, in this life, keep ourselves from sin all wholly and in full cleanness, as we shall be in heaven. But we may well, by grace, keep ourselves from the sins which would lead us to endless pain, as Holy Church teacheth us; and eschew venial sins, reasonably, with all our might. And if we, by our blindness and our wretchedness, at any time fall, we should readily rise, conscious of the sweet touching of grace; and wilfully amend us, in the teaching of the Holy Church, according as the sin is grievous, and go forth with God, in love. Neither should we, on one side, fall over low, turning to despair; nor, on the other, be over-reckless, as if we gave it no consideration. But meekly we should recognize our feebleness, realizing that we could not stand for the twinkling of an eye except by keeping of grace; and reverently cling to God, in him only trusting. For on one wise is the beholding of God, and other wise is the beholding of man. It belongeth to man meekly to accuse himself; and it belongeth to the proper goodness of our Lord God courteously to excuse man.

These are the two parts that were shewed in the twofold regard with which the Lord beheld the falling of his beloved servant. The one was shewed outward, full meekly and mildly, with great ruth and pity; the other inward, of endless love. And right thus, our Lord willeth that we accuse ourselves willingly and truthfully, seeing and knowing our falling, and all the harm that cometh thereof; seeing and realizing that we can never restore it; and therewith that we willingly and truly see and know the everlasting love which he hath for us, and his plenteous mercy. To see and know both parts together, thus graciously, is the meek accusing that our good Lord asketh of us. He himself worketh it, where it is—in the lower part of man's life. This was shewed in his outward regard; in which shewing I saw two elements: one is the rueful falling of man: the other is the worshipful redemption that our Lord hath made for man. The other regard, that was shewed inwardly, was of a much higher kind, and all a unity. For the life and the power that we have in our lower part is from the higher; and it cometh down to us by grace, by way of the kind love of the self. Between the one regard and the other there is no barrier, because it is all one love. This one blessed love now hath in us a double working. For in our lower part there are pains and passions, ruths and pities, mercies and forgivenesses, and other such, that are profitable. In our higher part are none of these, but all one high love and marvellous joy; in which marvellous joy, all pains are highly restored. And in this our good Lord shewed not only our excusing, but also the worshipful nobility that he shall bring us to; turning all our blame into endless worship.

THE FIFTY-THIRD CHAPTER

The kindness of God assigneth no blame to the chosen, for in these is a godly will that never consents to sin; the mercy of God must be knit to them, and a substance preserved in them that may never be separated from him

Thus I saw that it is his will for us to realize that he taketh no harder the falling of any creature that shall be saved than he took the falling of Adam; who, we know, was endlessly loved and surely kept in the time of all his need; and now is blissfully restored in high over-passing joy. For our Lord God is so good, so gentle and so courteous that he can never assign failure to those in whom he shall be ever blessed and praised.

In all this that I have now told, my desire was answered in part, and my great fear somewhat eased, by the lovely gracious shewing of our Lord God; in which I saw and understood full surely that in every soul which shall be saved there is a godly will that never assented to sin, nor ever shall. This will is so good that it may never will evil, but evermore, continually, it willeth good and worketh good in the sight of God. Our Lord willeth that we know this in faith and belief; and especially, that in truth we have all this blessed will whole and safe in our Lord Jesus Christ. For this same kind, with which heaven shall be filled, must needs be according to God's righteousness, so knit and oned in him, that in it must be preserved a substance which never could nor should be separated from him. And all this through his own good will and his endless foreseeing purpose. But notwithstanding this rightful knitting and this endless oneing, the redemption and the again-buying of mankind is needful and speedful in everything, in that it is done for the same purpose and the same end. This Holy Church, in our faith, teacheth us. For I saw that God never began to love mankind; but right as mankind shall be in endless bliss, bringing to fulfilment the joy of God relative to his works: right so the same mankind hath been, in the foreknowledge of God, known and loved from without-beginning, according to his righteous plan. And by the endless purpose and decision and the full accord of the Trinity, the second Person was to be the ground and head of this fair human kind; of him we are all sprung, in him we are all enclosed, to him we shall all go; finding in him our full heaven in everlasting joy; according to the foreseeing purpose of all the blessed Trinity from without-beginning. For ere that he made us, he loved us; and when we were made we loved him. This is a love made of the divine substantial love of the Holy Ghost, mighty by reason of the Power of the Father, wise in the consciousness of the Wisdom of the Son. Thus is man's soul made by God, and in the same moment knit to God. I understand that man's soul is made of naught; that is to say, it is made, but not from anything that is made—as when God would make man's body he took the slime of the earth, which is a material mingled and blended, out of all bodily things: thereof he made man's body. But for the making of man's soul, he would use naught at all: he simply made it. And thus is made-kind rightfully oned to the Maker, who is substantial unmade-kind: that is, God. Whence it is that there nor may be nor shall be anything at all between God and man's soul.

In this endless love, man's soul is kept whole; as all the matter of the Revelations meaneth and sheweth; in which endless love we are led and preserved by God, and never shall be lost. For he willeth that we know that our soul is a life; which life, by his goodness and his grace, shall last in heaven without end; him loving, him thanking, him praising. And right the same as we are to be without end, right so we were treasured in God, and hid: known and loved from without-beginning. Therefore he willeth us to know that the noblest thing that ever he made is mankind; and the fullest substance and the highest power is the blessed soul of Christ. Furthermore he meaneth us to know that this best beloved soul was preciously knit to him in the making of it: and the knot is so subtle and so strong that this soul is oned unto God: in which oneing it is made endlessly holy. Furthermore he meaneth us to know that all the souls that shall be saved in heaven without end, are knit in this knot and oned in this oneing, and made holy in this holiness.

THE FIFTY-FOURTH CHAPTER

We ought to rejoice that God dwelleth in our soul, and our soul in God; so that between God and our soul is nothing, but it is, as it were, all God. And how faith is ground of all power in our soul, by the Holy Ghost

AND through the great endless love that God hath to all mankind, he maketh no division, in love, between the blessed soul of Christ and the least soul that shall be saved. For it is full easy to believe and trust that the dwelling of the blessed soul of Christ is full high in the glorious Godhead. And truly, as I understood in our Lord's meaning, where the blessed soul of Christ is, there is the substance of all the souls that shall be saved by Christ.

Highly ought we to rejoice that God dwelleth in our soul; and much more highly ought we to rejoice that our soul dwelleth in God. Our soul is made to be God's dwelling-place; and the dwelling of our soul is God, which is unmade. A high understanding it is inwardly, to see and to know that God, who is our Maker, dwelleth in our soul. And a higher understanding it is, and more inwardly, to see and to know that our soul, that is made, dwelleth in God in substance. Of which substance, by God, we are what we are. And I saw no difference between God and our substance; but as it were all God. And yet my understanding took it that our substance is in God; that is to say, that God is God, and our substance is a creature in God.

For the almighty Truth of the Trinity, he is our Father; for he made us and keepeth us in him. And the deep Wisdom of the Trinity is our Mother, in whom we are enclosed. And the high Goodness of the Trinity is our Lord; and in him we are enclosed, and he in us. We are enclosed in the Father; and we are enclosed in the Son; and we are enclosed in the

Holy Ghost. And the Father is enclosed in us, and the Son is enclosed in us, and the Holy Ghost is enclosed in us: all-mightiness, all-wisdom, and all-goodness—one God, one Lord.

And our faith is a power that cometh from our kind substance into our sensual soul, by the Holy Ghost. In which power, all our virtues come to us; for without that, no man may receive virtues. For it is naught else but a right understanding, with true belief and sure trust, of our being: that we are in God and he in us—which we see not. And this power, with all other that God hath ordained to us coming therein, worketh in us great things. For Christ is mercifully working in us, and we are graciously disposed to him, through the gift and power of the Holy Ghost. This working maketh that we are Christ's children, and Christian in living.

THE FIFTY-FIFTH CHAPTER

Christ is our way, leading and presenting us to the Father. And as soon as the soul is infused in the body, mercy and grace work. And how the second Person took our sensuality to save us from a double death

AND thus Christ is our way; us surely leading in his laws. And Christ, in his body, mightily beareth us up into heaven. For I saw that Christ, us all having in him—that shall be saved by him—worshipfully presenteth his father in heaven with us. Which present with full thanks his Father receiveth, and courteously giveth it unto his Son, Jesus Christ. Which gift and working is joy to the Father, bliss to the Son, and liking to the Holy Ghost. And of all things that belong to us, it is most liking to our Lord that we rejoice in this joy which is in the blessed Trinity because of our salvation.

And this was seen in the ninth shewing, where it speaketh

more of this matter. And notwithstanding all our feeling—woe or weal—God willeth that we understand and believe that we are more verily in heaven than in earth. Our faith cometh from the kind love of our soul, and from the clear light of our reason, and from the steadfast mind which we have of God, in our first making. And what time our soul is breathed into our body—in which we are made sensual, at once mercy and grace begin to work, having of us care and keeping with pity and love. In which working, the Holy Ghost formeth, in our faith, hope that we shall come again to our substance up above, having increase and filled full of the power of Christ, through the Holy Ghost.

Thus I understood that the sensuality is grounded in kind, in mercy and in grace. Which ground enableth us to receive gifts that lead us to endless life. For I saw full surely that our substance is in God; and I also saw that in our sensuality God is. For in the point where our soul is made sensual, there in the same point is the city of God, ordained for him from without-beginning. Into which city he cometh, and never shall remove from it. For God is never out of the soul, in which he shall dwell blessedly without end. And this was seen in the sixteenth shewing, where it saith: "The place that Jesus taketh in the soul, he shall never remove from it."

And all the gifts that God may give to the creature, he hath given to his Son, Jesus, for us. Which gifts he, dwelling in us, hath enclosed in him, unto the time that we shall be full grown; our soul with our body, and our body with our soul—each of them taking help of the other, until we are brought up to our full stature, according to the workings of Kind. And then, in this ground of Kind, the Holy Ghost, with working of mercy, graciously breatheth into us gifts leading to endless life.

And thus was my understanding led, of God, to see in him and to realize, to understand and to know, that our soul is a made trinity, like to the unmade blessed Trinity, known and loved from without-beginning; and in the making, oned to the Maker, as it is beforesaid. This sight was full sweet and marvellous to behold, peaceful and restful, secure and delightful. And because of the worshipful oneing that was thus made, of God, between the soul and the body, it must needs be that man's kind should be restored from a double death. Which restoring might never be, until the time that the second Person in the Trinity had taken the lower part of man's kind, to whom that higher part was oned, in the first making. And these two parts were in Christ—the higher and the lower; which is but one soul. The higher part was ever in peace with God, in full joy and bliss; the lower part, which is sensuality, suffered for the salvation of mankind.

And these two parts were seen and felt in the eighth shewing; in which my mind was filled full of feeling and mind of Christ's passion and his dying. And furthermore with this was a subtle feeling and a secret inward sight of the high part. And that was shewed in the same time in which I could not, in spite of the friendly offer, look up into heaven. And that was because of that same mighty beholding of the inward life. Which inward life is that high substance, that precious soul which is endlessly in joy of the Godhead.

THE FIFTY-SIXTH CHAPTER

It is easier to know God than our soul; for God is to us nearer. And therefore, if we will have knowing of it, we must seek into God. And he willeth that we desire to have knowledge of kind, mercy and grace

AND thus I saw full surely that it is readier to us and more easy, to come to the knowing of God than to know our own soul. For our soul is so deep-grounded in God and so endlessly treasured, that we may not come to the knowing thereof until we have, first, knowing of God, who is the Maker; to whom it is oned. But notwithstanding I saw that we have, of our fullness, the desire wisely and truly to know our own soul; whereby we are learned to seek it where it is: and that is, in God. And thus, by the gracious leading of the Holy Ghost, we shall know them both in one. Whether we are stirred to know God or our own soul, both stirrings are good and true.

God is nearer to us than our own soul. For he is the ground in whom our soul standeth; and he is the mean that keepeth the substance and sensuality together, so that they shall never part. For our soul sitteth in God in very rest; and our soul standeth in God in sure strength; and our soul is kindly rooted in God in endless love. And therefore, if we will to have knowing of our soul, and communing and dalliance therewith, it behoveth to seek into our Lord God, in whom it is enclosed. And of this enclosing I saw and understood more in the sixteenth shewing, as I shall say.

And as regards our substance, it may rightly be called our soul. And as regards our sensuality, it may rightly be called our soul. And that is, by the oneing that it hath in God. That worshipful city that our Lord Jesus sitteth in, it is our sensuality, in which he is enclosed. And our kindly substance is enclosed in Jesus; sitting, with the blessed soul of Christ, in rest in the Godhead. And I saw full surely that it must needs be that we should be in longing and in penance, until the time that we be led so deep into God, that we verily and truly know our own soul.

And soothly I saw that into this high deepness our good Lord himself leadeth us, in the same love wherewith he made us, and in the same love wherewith he bought us, by mercy and grace, through the power of his blessed passion.

And notwithstanding all this, we may never come to the full knowing of God, until we know, first, clearly, our own soul. For until the time that it is in the fullness of its powers we cannot be all holy; and that is, until our sensuality, by virtue of Christ's passion, be brought up into the substance, with all the profits of our tribulation that our Lord shall make us to get, by mercy and grace.

I had, in part, touching: and it is grounded in kind. That is to say, our reason is grounded in God, who is substantial kindhood. Of this substantial kindhood, mercy and grace spring, and spread into us; working all things in fulfilling of our joy. These are our ground, in which we have our being, our increase and our fulfilling. For in kind we have our life and our being; and in mercy and grace we have our increase and our fulfilling. Here are three properties in one goodness; and wherever one worketh, all work, in the things which now belong to us. God willeth that we understand, desiring with all our heart and all our strength to have knowing of them, ever more and more unto the time that we shall be full filled. For fully to know them and clearly to see them is naught else but the endless joy and bliss that we shall have in heaven; which God willeth that we begin here, in the knowing of his love. For by our reason alone we cannot profit, unless we have, equally therewith, mind and love. Nor can we be saved merely in that we have our kindly ground in God; unless we have, coming of the same ground, mercy and grace. For of these three workings, all together, we receive all our goods. Of which the first is goods of kind. For in our first making God gave us much good; and also greater goods, such as we could receive only in our spirit. But his foreseeing purpose, in his endless wisdom, willed that we should be double.

THE FIFTY-SEVENTH CHAPTER

In our substance we are full: in our sensuality we fail—which God will restore by mercy and grace. And how our kind, which is the higher part, is knit to God in the making: and God, Jesus, is knit to our kind in the lower part, in our flesh taking: and of faith spring other virtues: and Mary is our Mother

AND in respect of our substance, he made us so noble and so rich that ever more we work his will and his worship. (Where I say "we", it meaneth "man that shall be saved".) For truly I saw that we are whom he loveth and do what him liketh, lastingly and without any stint. And of this great richness and of this high nobility, virtues, according to measure, come to our soul, what time it is knit to our body. In which knitting we are made sensual. And thus in our substance we are full, and in our sensuality we fail. Which failing God willeth to restore and fulfil by the working of mercy and grace, plenteously flowing into us from his own kind goodness. And thus this kind goodness ensureth that mercy and grace worketh in us. And the kind goodness that we have of him enableth us to receive the working of mercy and grace.

I saw that our kind is in God, wholly; in which he maketh diversities, flowing out of him, to work his will. Whomso kind keepeth, and mercy and grace restore and fulfil, of these none shall perish. For our kind which is the higher part is knit to God in the making; and God is knit to our kind which is the lower part, in taking of our flesh. And thus in Christ our two kinds are oned; for Christ is comprehended in the Trinity, in whom our higher part is grounded and rooted; and our lower part the second Person hath taken— which kind was first prepared for him. For I saw full truly that all the works that God hath done, or ever shall, were full known to him and before-seen, from without-beginning. And for love he made mankind; and for the same love, himself would become man.

The next good that we receive is our faith; in which our profiting beginneth. And it cometh, this high largesse, of our kind substance, into our sensual soul. And it is grounded in us, and we in it, through the kind goodness of God, by the working of mercy and grace. Of this working come all our goods whereby we are directed and brought to salvation.

For the commandments of God come therein; concerning which we ought to have a two-fold understanding. One is, that we should understand and know what his biddings are, and how to love them and keep them. The other is that we should know his forbiddings—how to hate them and refuse them. For in these two is all our working comprehended.

Also in our faith come the seven sacraments, each following other in the order in which God hath instituted them for us: and every sort of virtue. For the same virtues that we have received of our substance, as given to us in kind, out of the goodness of God—these same virtues are given to us by the working of mercy, renewed in grace through the Holy Ghost. Which virtues and gifts become our treasure in Jesus Christ. For in that same time that God knit himself to our body in the maiden's womb, he took our sensual soul. In taking which, having enclosed us all in himself, he oned it to our substance. In this oneing he was perfect man; for Christ, having knit in himself every man that shall be saved, is perfect man.

Thus our Lady is our Mother in whom we are all enclosed; and, of her, born in Christ. For she that is Mother of our Saviour is Mother of all that are saved in our Saviour. And our Saviour is our true Mother, in whom we are endlessly borne; and we shall never come out of him.

Plenteously, fully and sweetly was this shewed. And it is spoken of in the first shewing, where it said: "We are all in him enclosed, and he is enclosed in us". And it is spoken of in the sixteenth shewing, where it saith he sitteth in the soul. For it is his liking to reign in our understanding blissfully, and to sit in our soul restfully, and to dwell in our soul endlessly; working us all into him. In which working he willeth that we be his helpers, giving to him all our mind; learning his laws, keeping his counsels, desiring that all be done that he doeth, truly trusting in him. For verily I saw that our substance is in God.

THE FIFTY-EIGHTH CHAPTER

God was never displeased with his chosen Wife; and of three properties in the Trinity, Fatherhood, Motherhood and Lordship: and how our substance is in each Person, but our sensuality is in Christ alone

GOD the blissful Trinity—which is everlasting Being, right as he is endless from without-beginning, right so it was in his endless purpose to make man's kind. Which fair kind was first prepared for his own Son, the second Person. And whenso he would, by full accord of all the Trinity, he made all of us at once. And in our making he knit us and oned us to himself. By which oneing we are kept as clean and as noble as we were made. By virtue of that same precious oneing, we love our Maker and like him, praise him and thank him and endlessly rejoice in him. And this is the working which is wrought continually in every soul that shall be saved—the aforesaid godly will.

And thus, in our making, God almighty is our kindly Father: and God all-wisdom is our kindly Mother: with the love and goodness of the Holy Ghost; which is all one God, one Lord. And in the knitting and the oneing he is our very true Spouse, and we his loved wife and his fair maiden. With which wife he was never displeased; for he saith: "I love thee, and thou lovest me, and our love shall never be parted in two."

I beheld the working of all the blessed Trinity. In which beholding I saw and understood these three properties: the property of the Fatherhood, and the property of the Motherhood, and the property of the Lordship—in one God. In our Father almighty we have our keeping and our bliss, in respect of our kindly substance (which is applied to us by our creation), from without-beginning. And in the second Person, in understanding and wisdom, we have our keeping in respect of our sensuality, our restoring and our saving. (For he is our Mother, Brother and Saviour.) And in our good Lord the Holy Ghost we have our rewarding and our enrichment for our living and our travail: which, of his high plenteous grace, and in his marvellous courtesy, endlessly surpasseth all that we desire.

For all our life is in three. In the first we have our being: and in the second we have our increasing: and in the third we have our fulfilling. The first is kind: the second is mercy: the third is grace. For the first: I saw and understood that the high might of the Trinity is our Father, and the deep wisdom of the Trinity is our Mother, and the great love of the Trinity is our Lord. And all these we have in kind and in our substantial making.

And furthermore, I saw that the second Person, who is our Mother substantially—the same very dear Person is now become our Mother sensually. For of God's making we are double: that is to say, substantial and sensual. Our substance is that higher part which we have in our Father, God almighty. And the second Person of the Trinity is our Mother in kind, in our substantial making—in whom we are grounded and rooted; and he is our Mother of mercy. in taking our sensuality. And thus "our Mother" meaneth for us different manners of his working, in whom our parts are kept unseparated. For in our Mother Christ, we have profit and increase; and in mercy he re-formeth and restoreth us: and by the power of his passion, his death and his uprising, oned us to our substance. Thus worketh our Mother in mercy to all his beloved children who are docile and obedient to him.

And grace worketh with mercy; and especially in two properties, as it was shewed. Which working belongeth to the third Person, the Holy Ghost; he worketh by rewarding and giving. Rewarding is a gift—fulfilment of a pledge—that the Lord maketh to them that have laboured; and giving is a courteous working, of grace, full filling and surpassing all that is deserved by creatures.

Thus in our Father, God almighty, we have our being. And in our Mother of mercy we have our reforming and our restoring; in whom our parts are oned, and all made perfect man; and by the enriching and giving, in grace, of the Holy Ghost, we are full filled. And our substance is in our Father, God almighty; and our substance is in our Mother, God all-wisdom; and our substance is in our Lord God the Holy Ghost, all-goodness. For our substance is whole in each Person of the Trinity, which is one God. But our sensuality is only in the second Person, Christ Jesus: in whom is the Father and the Holy Ghost. And in him and by him we are mightily taken out of hell, and out of the wretchedness in earth, and worshipfully brought up into heaven; and blissfully oned to our substance, increased in richness and nobility, by the power of Christ and by the grace and working of the Holy Ghost.

THE FIFTY-NINTH CHAPTER

Wickedness is turned to bliss, in the chosen, by mercy and grace: for the property of God is to do good against ill, by Jesus, our Mother in kind grace; and the highest soul in virtue is the meekest—of which ground we have all other virtues

AND all this bliss we have by mercy and grace; which sort of bliss we might never have had or known, if that property of goodness which is in God (whereby we have this bliss) had been cancelled out. For wickedness hath been permitted to rise up contrary to the goodness. But the goodness of mercy and grace stood contrary against that wickedness, and turned all to goodness and worship—unto all that shall be saved. For it is the property in God which doeth good against evil.

Thus Jesus Christ, who doeth good against evil, is our very Mother. We have our being of him, there, where the ground of Motherhood beginneth; with all the sweet keeping of love that endlessly followeth. As truly as God is our Father, so truly is God our Mother. And that shewed he in all, and especially in these sweet words where he saith "I it am". That is to say:

> I it am: the might and the goodness of the Fatherhood. I it am: the wisdom and the kindness of Motherhood. I it am: the light and the grace that is all blessed love. I it am, the Trinity. I it am, the Unity. I it am the high sovereign Goodness of all manner thing. I it am that maketh thee to love. I it am that maketh thee to long. I it am, the endless fulfilling of all true desires.

For where the soul is highest, noblest and most worshipful, there it is lowest, meekest and mildest. And of this substantial ground we have all our virtues, in our sensuality, by gift of kind, and by helping and speeding of mercy and grace —without which we cannot profit. Our high Father almighty God, who is Being, he knew us and loved us from before-any-time. Of which knowing, in his full marvellous deep Charity, by the foreseeing endless counsel of all the blessed Trinity, he willed that the second Person should become our Mother, our Brother, and our Saviour. Whereof it followeth that as truly as God is our Father, so truly is God our Mother. Our Father willeth, our Mother worketh, our good Lord the Holy Ghost confirmeth. And therefore it belongeth to us to love our God, in whom we have our being; him reverently thanking and praising for our making; mightily praying to our Mother for mercy and pity, and to our Lord the Holy Ghost for help and grace. For in these three is all our life—kind, mercy and grace; whereof we have mildness, patience and pity, and hating of sin and wickedness. For it belongeth properly to the virtues to hate sin and wickedness.

And thus is Jesus our true Mother in kind, of our first making; and he is our true Mother in grace by his taking of our made kind. All the fair working and all the sweet kindly offices of most dear Motherhood are appropriated to the second Person. For in him we have this godly will whole and secure without end, both in kind and in grace, of his own proper goodness. I understand three types of beholding of Motherhood in God. The first is the ground of making of our kind. The second is the taking of our kind—and there beginneth the Motherhood of grace. The third is Motherhood in working. And therein is a forth-spreading, by the same grace, of a length and breadth, of a height and a deepness without end. And all is one love.

THE SIXTIETH CHAPTER

How we are brought again and forthspread, by mercy and grace, of our sweet, kind and ever-loving Mother Jesus; and of the properties of motherhood. But Jesus is our true Mother, feeding us, not with milk, but with himself: opening his side unto us, and challenging all our love

BUT now it behoveth me to say a little more of this forth-spreading, as I understand it in the meaning of our Lord: how that we are brought again by the Motherhood of mercy and grace into the kindly state, wherein we were made, by the Motherhood of kind love; which kind love never leaveth us.

Our kind Mother, our gracious Mother—for he would all wholly become our Mother in all things—he made the ground of his work to be full low and full mildly in the Maiden's womb. And that shewed he in the first shewing, where he brought that meek maiden before the eye of my understanding, in the simple stature, as she was when she conceived. That is to say: our high God, the sovereign Wisdom of all, in this lowly place he arrayed him and made him all ready; in our poor flesh, himself to do the service and office of Motherhood, in all things.

The mother's service is nearest, readiest and surest; nearest: for it is most of kind; readiest: for it is most of love; surest: for it is most of truth. This office no one might nor could ever do to the full, except he alone. We know that all our mothers bear us to pain and to dying; a strange thing, that! But our true Mother Jesus, he alone beareth us to joy and to endless living; blessed may he be! Thus he sustaineth us within him, in love and in travail unto the full time in which he willed to suffer the sharpest throes and most grievous pains that ever were, or ever shall be; and he died at the last. Yet all this might not fully satisfy his marvellous love. And that shewed he in these high overpassing words of love: "If I could suffer more, I would suffer more". He could no more die, but he would not cease working.

Wherefore it behoveth him to feed us; for the very dear love of motherhood hath made him our debtor. The mother can give her child to suck of her milk. But our precious Mother Jesus, he can feed us with himself; and doth, full courteously and tenderly, with the Blessed Sacrament, that is the precious food of true life. And with all the sweet sacraments he sustaineth us full mercifully and graciously. And this was his meaning in those blessed words, where he said: "I it am that Holy Church preacheth to thee and teacheth thee"; that is to say, all the health and the life of the sacraments. "All the power and the grace of my word, all the goodness that is ordained to thee in Holy Church, I it am."

The mother can lay her child tenderly to her breast. But our tender Mother Jesus can lead us, homely, into his blessed breast, by his sweet open side; and shew us there, in part, the Godhead and the joys of heaven, with a ghostly sureness of endless bliss. And that shewed he in the ninth Revelation, giving the same understanding in the sweet words where he saith: "Lo, how I love thee"—looking into his blessed side, rejoicing.

This fair lovely word *Mother*, it is so sweet and so kind in itself, that it cannot truly be said to any nor of any, but to him and of him who is very Mother of life and of all. To the property of Motherhood belongeth kind love, wisdom and knowing; and it is God. For though it is true that our bodily forthbringing is but little, lowly and simple in comparison with our ghostly forthbringing; yet it is he that doeth the first in the creatures by whom it is done. The kind loving mother understandeth and knoweth the need of her child. She keepeth it full tenderly, as the kind and condition of motherhood will. And ever as it waxeth in age and in stature, she changeth her way of working, but not her love. And when it is come to a more advanced age, she suffereth it to be chastised, for the breaking down of vices, and to make the child receive virtues and grace. This work, with all that is fair and good, our Lord doeth it, in those by whom it is done.

Thus he is our Mother in kind by the working of grace in the lower part, for the sake of the higher. And he willeth that we know it. For he willeth to have all our love fastened to him. And in this I saw that all the debts that we owe, by God's bidding, to fatherhood and motherhood are fulfilled in true loving of God. Which blessed love Christ worketh in us. And this was shewed in everything; but especially in the high plenteous words, where he saith: "I it am that thou lovest".

THE SIXTY-FIRST CHAPTER

Jesus useth more tenderness in our ghostly bringing forth: though he suffereth us to fall, for the knowing of our wretchedness, he hastily raiseth us: not breaking his love because of our trespass, for he cannot suffer his child to perish; for he willeth that we have the quality of a child, fleeing to him always in our necessity

AND in our ghostly forthbringing he useth more tenderness (without any comparison) by as much as our soul is of more price in his sight. He kindleth our understanding, he prepareth our ways, he comforteth our soul, he enlighteneth our heart; and giveth us, in part, a knowing and loving in his blissful Godhead, with gracious mind of his sweet manhood and his blessed passion, with courteous marvelling at his high surpassing goodness. And he maketh us to love all that he loveth, for his love; and to be well satisfied with him, and with all his works.

And when we fall, hastily he raiseth us by the clasping of his love and the touching of his grace. And when we are strengthened by his sweet working, then we deliberately choose him, by his grace, to be his servants and his lovers, lastingly without end. And yet, after this, he suffereth some of us to fall more hard and more grievously than ever we did before—or so it would seem. And then we think (for we are not all wise) that all we have begun is brought to naught. But it is not so. For we needs must fall; and we needs must see it. For if we fell not, we should never know how feeble and how wretched we are, of ourselves. Nor should we know so fully the marvellous love of our Maker. For we shall truly see in heaven, without end, that we have grievously sinned in this life. Yet notwithstanding this, we shall truly see that we were never hurt in his love; nor were any the less precious in his sight. By the experience of this falling we shall have an high and a marvellous knowing of love in God, without end. For staunch and marvellous is that love which cannot or will not be broken because of trespass.

This was one understanding that was profitable. Another is the lowliness and meekness that we shall get by the sight of our falling. For thereby we shall highly be raised in heaven—to which we could never come without that meekness. And therefore we need to see it. For if we see it not, even though we fell, it would not profit us. Ordinarily, first we fall, and then we see it. And both are of the mercy of God. The mother may suffer her child to fall sometimes, and to be distressed in different ways, for its own profit. But she can never permit that any manner of peril come to her child, because of her love. And though, possibly, an earthly mother may suffer her child to perish, our heavenly Mother Jesus can never suffer us who are his children to perish. For he is almighty, all-wisdom and all-love: and so is none but he. Blessed may he be!

But oftentimes, when our falling and our wretchedness is shewed to us, we are so sore adread, and so greatly ashamed of ourselves, that we scarcely know where to put ourselves. Yet even then our courteous Mother willeth not that we flee away: nothing could be more displeasing to him. Rather, he willeth us to behave as a child. For when it is distressed and afraid, it runneth hastily to the mother. And if it can do naught else, it cryeth to the mother for help, with all its might. So will he have us behave as the meek child, saying thus: "My kind Mother, my gracious Mother, my most dear Mother, have mercy on me. I have made myself foul and unlike to thee; and I cannot or may not amend it but with thine help and grace." And if we do not feel eased at once, then we may be sure that he useth the way of a wise mother. For if he see that it is for our profit to mourn and to weep, he suffereth that, with ruth and pity—until the right time, out of love.

It is his will, then, that we behave as a child, who ever more kindly trusteth to the love of the mother, in weal and in woe. And he willeth that we betake us, mightily, to the faith of Holy Church; and find in her our most dear Mother, in solace and true understanding, with all the Communion of Saints. For a single person may often be broken—or so it seemeth to the self. But the whole Body of the Church was never broken, nor ever shall be, without end. And therefore a sure thing it is, a good and a gracious, to will, meekly and mightily, to be fastened and oned to our Mother Holy Church; that is, Christ Jesus. For the flood of mercy that is his most dear blood and precious water is plenteous to make us fair and clean. The blessed wounds of our Saviour are open, and rejoice to heal us. The sweet gracious hands of our Mother are ready and diligent about us.

For he, in all this working, fulfilleth the office of a kind nurse that hath naught else to do but to attend to the well-being of her child. It is his office to save us: it is his worship to do it, and it is his will that we know it. For he willeth that we love him sweetly, and trust in him meekly and mightily. And this shewed he in these gracious words, "I keep thee full surely".

THE SIXTY-SECOND CHAPTER

The love of God suffereth never his chosen to lose time: for all their trouble is turned into endless joy; and how we are all obliged to God for kindness and for grace; for every kind is in man: and we need not seek out to know various kinds, but Holy Church alone

IN that time he shewed our frailty and our falling, our being broken and despoiled, our being crossed and accused: and all our woe, as far forth as methought could ever befall us in this life. But with it he shewed his blessed might, his blessed wisdom, his blessed love—that he keepeth us, in this time, as tenderly and as sweetly (for his worship) and as surely unto our salvation, as he doth when we are most in solace and comfort. And with that he raiseth us ghostly and highly in heaven; and turneth all to his worship and to our joy, without end.

For his precious love never suffereth us to lose time; and all this is of the kind goodness of God, by the working of grace. God is kind in his Being. That is to say: the Goodness which is Kind, is God. He is the Ground: he is the Substance: he is the very thing called Kindness. And he is the very Father and the very Mother of kinds. And all kinds that he hath made to flow out of him to work his will, they must be restored and brought again into him, by the salvation of man, through the working of grace. For of all the kinds that he hath set in various creatures separately, only in man is all the whole—in fullness and in power, in beauty and in goodness, in royalty and nobility: in all manner of eminence, of preciousness and honour.

Here may we see that we are all indebted to God for kind, and we are indebted to God for grace. Here may we see that we need not go very far out of our way to get to know various kinds, but merely to Holy Church, into our Mother's breast; that is to say, into our own soul, where our Lord dwelleth. And there shall we find all; now in faith and in understanding, and afterwards truly in himself, clearly, in bliss. But let no man nor woman understand this of himself, individually; for it is not so. This fair kind, it is general; it is our precious Mother, Christ. For him was this fair kind prepared: for the worship and nobility of man's making and for the joy and the bliss of man's salvation; just as he saw, understood and knew it, from without-beginning.

THE SIXTY-THIRD CHAPTER

Sin is more painful than hell: and vile and harmful to kind; but grace saveth kind and destroyeth sin; the children of Jesus are not yet all born; they pass not the stature of childhood, but live in feebleness until they come to heaven, where joys are ever new, ever beginning, without end

HERE may we see that it truly belongeth to us, of kind, to hate sin. For kind is all good and fair in itself. And grace was sent out to save kind and keep kind; and destroy sin and bring again fair kind into the blessed place whence it came (that is, God), with more nobleness and worship, by the virtuous working of grace. For it shall be seen before God, by all his Holy Ones, in joy without end.

Yet kind hath been tried in the fire of tribulation, and in it was found no lack nor defect. Thus are kind and grace one accord. For grace is God, and unmade Kind is God. He is two, in manner of working (but one in love): and neither of them worketh without the other—they may not be parted. And when we, by the mercy of God and with his help, accord ourselves to kind and to grace, we shall see truly that sin is worse, more vile and more painful than hell—there is no comparison; it is contrary to our fair kind. For as truly as sin is unclean, as truly sin is unkind. All this is a horrible thing to see for the loving soul that would be all fair and shining in the sight of God, as kind and grace teach.

But let us not be adread of this, except in as much as dread may speed us; but meekly make we our moan to our most dear Mother. And he shall all besprinkle us in his precious blood, and make our soul full soft and full mild, and heal us to full fairness in the process of time—for thus it is most worship to him, and joy to us without end.

And of this sweet fair working he shall never cease nor stint himself until all his most dear children be born and brought forth. And that shewed he where he gave the understanding of the ghostly thirst, which is the love-longing that shall last till doomsday.

Thus in our true Mother Jesus our life is grounded, in the foreseeing wisdom of himself from without-beginning, with the high might of the Father and the sovereign goodness of the Holy Ghost. And in the taking of our kind he quickened us; and in his blessed dying upon the cross he bore us to endless life. And from that time, and now, he feedeth us and furthereth us, and ever shall until doomsday: right as the high sovereign kindness of Motherhood willeth, and the kindly need of childhood demandeth.

Fair and sweet is our heavenly Mother in the sight of our soul; precious and lovely are the gracious children in the sight of our heavenly Mother, with mildness and meekness and all the fair virtues that belong, in kind, to children. For kindly the children despair not of the mother's love, kindly the child presumeth not of itself, kindly the child loveth the mother and each one of them the other. These are the fair virtues (with all others that are like to them) wherewith our heavenly Mother is served and pleased. And I understood that there is no higher stature in this life than childhood—in the feebleness and failing of might and understanding—until the time that our gracious Mother hath brought us up to our Father's bliss. And there shall truly be made known to us his meaning, in the sweet words where he saith: "All shall be well; and thou shalt see it thyself that all manner thing shall be well."

THE SIXTY-FOURTH CHAPTER

The fifteenth Revelation. The absence of God in this life is full great pain to us, apart from other travail; but we shall suddenly be taken from all pain, having Jesus for our Mother, and our patient abiding is greatly pleasing to God; and God's will is that we take our distress lightly, for love, believing ourselves always on the point of being delivered

AND then shall the bliss of our Motherhood in Christ be begun anew in the joys of our Father, God. Which new beginning shall last without end. This new beginning I understood thus: that all his blessed children, who are come out of him by kind, should be brought again into him by grace.

Before this time, I had, of God's gift, great longing and desire to be delivered of this world and of this life. For oftentimes I beheld the woe that is here, and the weal and the blessed being that is there. And even if there had been no pain in this life, but the absence of our Lord, it seemed to me, sometimes, that it was more than I might bear. And this made me to mourn, and earnestly to long; and also because of my own wretchedness, sloth and weariness—that it liked me not to live and to travail as it fell to me to do.

And to all this our Lord answered, for comfort and patience, and said these words:

Suddenly thou shalt be taken from all thy pain, from all thy sickness, from all thy distress and from all thy woe. And thou shalt come up above, and thou shalt have me for thy meed, and thou shalt be filled full of joy and bliss. And thou shalt never more have any manner of pain, nor any manner of sickness, nor any manner of disliking, nor wanting of will; but ever joy and bliss without end. Why then should it grieve thee to suffer a while, since it is my will, and for my worship?

And in this word "suddenly thou shalt be taken", I saw that God rewardeth man for the patience that he hath in abiding God's will and his time; and that man stretcheth his patience across the time of his living, through unknowing of the time of his passing. This is of great profit. For if man knew his time, he would not have patience over that time.

And also it is God's will, that while the soul is in the body, it should seem to it that it is ever on the point of being taken. For all this life and this longing that we have here is but a point. And when we be taken suddenly out of pain into bliss, then pain shall be naught.

And in this time I saw a body lying on the earth. Which body was a heavy, fearful sight, without shape or form—a bloated mass of stinking mud. And suddenly, out of this body sprang a full fair creature, a little child fully shapen and formed, swift and full of life and whiter than the lily: it quickly glided up into heaven. The bloated mass of the body betokeneth the great wretchedness of our mortal flesh; and the littleness of the child betokeneth the cleanness and the purity of our soul. And I thought: "With this body this child's fairness cannot remain: nor can any foulness of body dwell with this child".

It is full blissful for man to be taken from pain, more than for pain to be taken from man. For if pain be taken from us, it can come again. Therefore this is a sovereign comfort and a blissful beholding for a soul in longing, that we shall be taken from pain. For in this promise I saw the merciful compassion that our Lord hath in us, for our woe, and a courteous pledge of cleansing deliverance. For it is his will that we be comforted in overpassing joy. And that he shewed in these words: "And thou shalt come up above: and thou shalt have me for thy meed: and thou shalt be filled full of joy and bliss."

It is God's will that we set the point of our thought in this blissful beholding as oftentimes as we may and for as long a time keep ourselves therein, with his grace. For this is a blissful contemplation for the soul that is led of God; and it is full much to his worship, for the time that it lasteth.

And when we fall again to ourselves, by heaviness and ghostly blindness and feeling of pains ghostly and bodily, by reason of our frailty, it is God's will that we know that he hath not forgotten us. And so meaneth he in these words, and saith for comfort: "And thou shalt never more have pain in any manner: nor any manner of sickness, nor any manner of disliking, nor wanting of will; but ever joy and bliss. Why should it then grieve thee to suffer awhile, since it is my will and to my worship?" It is God's will that we take his promises and his comforting as fully and as mightily as we may. And also it is his will that we take our abidings and our distress as lightly as we may, and set them at naught. For the more lightly that we take them, and the less price that we set on them, for love, the less pain shall we have in feeling of them, and the more thanks and meed shall we have for them.

THE SIXTY-FIFTH CHAPTER

He that chooseth God, for love, with reverent meekness, is sure to be saved; which reverent meekness seeth the Lord to be marvellous great, and the self marvellous little; and it is God's will that we dread nothing but him, for the power of our enemy is locked in our Friend's hand; and therefore all that God doeth shall be of great liking to us

AND thus I understood that what man or woman deliberately chooseth God in this life, for love, may be sure that he is loved without end. Which endless love worketh in him that grace. For he willeth us to hold trustfully to this—that we be as sure, in hope, of the bliss of heaven whilst we are here, as we shall be, in certainty, when we are there. And ever the more liking and joy that we take in this sureness, with reverence and meekness, the better it liketh him. For this reverence that I mean (as it was shewed) is a holy courteous dread of our Lord, to which meekness is knit; and that is, that a creature see the Lord marvellous great, and herself marvellous little.

These virtues are had endlessly by the beloved of God. And they may now be seen and felt, in a measure, by the gracious presence of our Lord, when it is given. Which presence is most desirable, in everything. For it worketh that marvellous sureness, in true faith and steadfast hope, by the greatness of charity, in dread that is sweet and delightful. It is God's will that I see myself as much bound to him in love, as if all that he hath done he had done for me. And thus should every soul think in regard of his Lover. That is to say: the charity of God maketh in us such a unity, that, when it is truly seen, no man can part himself from another. And so each soul ought to think that God hath done for him all that he hath done.

And this sheweth he to make us to love him and like him, and nothing dread but him. For it is his will that we know that all the might of our enemy is locked in our Friend's hands. And therefore the soul that knoweth this surely, she shall dread only him whom she loveth. All other dreads—she setteth them among passions, bodily sickness and imaginations. And therefore, though we be in so much pain, woe and distress that it seemeth that we can think of naught but the state that we are in, or that we feel; as soon as we may, let us pass lightly over it, and set it at naught. And why? Because God willeth us to know that if we know him and love him and reverently dread him, we shall have peace and be in great rest; and all that he doeth shall be great liking to us. And this shewed our Lord in these words: "Why should it then grieve thee to suffer awhile, seeing it is my will and to my worship?"

Now have I told you of fifteen shewings, as God vouchsafed to minister them to my mind: renewed by lightings and touchings, I hope of the same Spirit that shewed them all. Of which fifteen shewings the first began early in the morning, about the hour of four. And they lasted, shewn in order full fair and surely, each following the other, until it was past three in the day.

THE SIXTY-SIXTH CHAPTER

The sixteenth Revelation. And it is the conclusion and confirmation of all fifteen; and of her frailty and mourning in distress, and her light speaking after the great comfort of Jesus—saying that she had raved; this, being said in her great sickness, I suppose was but venial sin

AND after this, the good Lord shewed the sixteenth Revelation, on the night following, as I shall say afterwards. Which sixteenth was the conclusion and confirmation of all the fifteen.

But first I needs must tell you about my feebleness, wretchedness and blindness. I have said (at the beginning, where it saith: "And in this, suddenly all my pain was taken from me") that of pain I had no grief nor distress as long as the fifteen shewings lasted. But at the end, all was hid again, and I saw no more. And then I felt that I would go on living: but then my sickness came again; first in my head, with a loud sound and a noise. And suddenly all my body was filled full of sickness, like as it was before. And I was as barren and as dry as if I had never had but the least comfort. And as a wretch I mourned grievously, in feeling my bodily pains, and for the failing of comfort, ghostly and bodily.

Then came a religious, a parson, to me; and asked me how I fared. And I said I had raved during the day. But he laughed loud and heartily. And I said that the cross that stood before my face—it seemed to me that it bled freely. With this word, the parson to whom I spake grew very serious, and was filled with wonder. And straightway I was sore ashamed and abashed at my recklessness. And I thought: "This man, that saw nothing thereof, taketh seriously the least word that I say". And when I saw that he took it so seriously and with such reverence, I grew greatly ashamed and desired to be shriven. But I could not tell the fault to a priest; "for", I thought, "how would a priest believe me, when I, by saying I raved, shewed myself not to believe our Lord God?" Notwithstanding this, I believed him truly during the time that I saw him, and at that time it was my will and meaning ever to do so, without end. But like a fool, I let this pass out of my mind. Alas, what a wretch I was! This was a great sin and a great unkindness, that out of folly, and for feeling of a little bodily pain, I so unwisely left, for the time, the comfort of all this blessed shewing of our Lord God.

Here may you see what I am of myself. But herein our courteous Lord would not leave me. And I lay still until night, trusting in his mercy; and then I began to sleep.

THE SIXTY-SEVENTH CHAPTER

Yet the Devil, after that, had great power to molest her, nigh unto death

AND in my sleep, at the beginning, it seemed as though the fiend set himself at my throat, thrusting his face close to mine—the face of a young man, long and incredibly lean: I never saw its like. Its colour was red, like the tile-stone fresh from the kiln, with black spots in it like freckles—dirtier than a tile-stone. His hair was red as rust, cut short in front, with side-locks hanging down his cheeks. He looked at me with a malignant grin, shewing his white teeth. And the more he grinned, the more ugly he seemed. Body or hands had he none, of true shape; but with his paws he held me by the throat, and would have stopped my breath and killed me; but he might not.

This ugly shewing alone was made whilst I slept: no other was shewn so. And in all this time, I trusted to be saved and kept by the mercy of God; and our courteous Lord gave me grace to wake.

I scarcely had any life in me. But the persons that were with me looked at me and wet my temples; and my heart began to take comfort. Immediately, a little smoke came in at the door, with a great heat and a foul stench. And then said I, "God bless us! Is all the place on fire?" For I thought it was a bodily fire that would burn us all to death. I asked them that were with me if they smelt any stench. They said "Nay," they smelt nothing. I said "Blessed be God". For then I understood that it was only the fiend, come to tempt me. Then straightway I betook me to what our Lord had shewed me on the same day, with all the faith of Holy Church (for I beheld both these as in one); and fled thereto, as to my comfort. And immediately all vanished away; and I was brought to great rest and peace, without sickness of body or dread of conscience.

THE SIXTY-EIGHTH CHAPTER

Of the worshipful city of the soul, which is so nobly created that it might no better be made: in which the Trinity joyeth everlastingly; and the soul can have rest in nothing but in God, who sitteth therein, ruling all things

AND then our good Lord opened my ghostly eye, and shewed me my soul in the midst of my heart. I saw the soul, so large as it were an endless world, and also as it were a blessed kingdom. And by the appointments that I saw therein, I understood that it is a worshipful city. In the midst of that city is our Lord Jesus, true God and true man, comely of person and tall of stature, the greatest bishop, most aweful king, Lord of highest honour. And I saw him arrayed in majesty and honour. He sitteth in the soul, established in peace and rest. And he ruleth and maintaineth heaven and earth and all that is. The manhood with the Godhead sitteth in rest; the Godhead ruleth and maintaineth without any instrument or labour. And the soul is all occupied with the blessed Godhead which is sovereign Might, sovereign Wisdom, sovereign Goodness.

The place that Jesus taketh in our soul—he shall never remove therefrom without end. For in us is his homeliest home, and his endless dwelling. And in this he shewed the liking that he hath in the making of a creature. For well as the Father might make a creature, and well as the Son might make a creature; just so well the Holy Ghost willed that man's soul should be made. And so it was done. And therefore the blissful Trinity rejoiceth without end in the making of man's soul. For he saw from without-beginning what would please him without end.

All things that he hath made shew his Lordship; as understanding was given, in the same time, by the example of a creature who is brought to see the great nobility of the kingdoms belonging to a Lord. And when the creature had seen all the nobility below, then, marvelling, it was moved to seek up above into that high place where the Lord dwelleth (knowing by its reason that his dwelling must be in the worthiest place).

And thus I understood truly that our soul may never have rest in anything that is beneath itself. And when it cometh above all creatures into itself, yet it cannot dwell in the beholding of itself; but all its beholding is blissfully set in God who is the Maker, dwelling therein; for in man's soul is his true dwelling. And the highest light and the brightest shining of the city is the glorious love of our Lord God, as to my sight. And what can make us more rejoice in God than to see in him that he rejoiceth in us, the highest of all his works?

For I saw in the same shewing that if the blessed Trinity could have made man's soul any the better, any the fairer, any the nobler than it was made, he would not have been fully pleased with the making of man's soul. But because he made man's soul as fair, as good and as precious as he could make a creature, therefore the blessed Trinity is fully pleased without end in the making of man's soul. And it is his will that our hearts be mightily raised above the depths of the earth and all vain sorrows, and rejoice in him.

This was a delightful sight and a restful shewing, that is without end. And the beholding of this, while we are here, is full pleasant to God and full great speed to us. And the soul that thus beholdeth—the sight maketh it like to him that is beheld, and oneth it to him in rest and in peace, by his grace. And this was a special joy and bliss to me—that I saw him sitting. For the sureness of sitting shewed endless dwelling. And he gave me to know truly that it was he who had shewed me all before.

And when I had beheld this with close attention, then shewed our Lord words, full meekly without voice and without opening of lips, just as he had done before, and said full sweetly:

> Know it now well that it was no raving that thou sawest today. But take it and believe it and keep thee therein, and comfort thee therewith, and trust thereto; and thou shalt not be overcome.

These last words were said for learning of full true sureness that it is our Lord Jesus that shewed me all. And just as in the first words that our Lord shewed, he said (meaning his blessed passion), "Herewith is the fiend overcome": just so in the last words he said, with full true faithfulness (meaning us all), "Thou shalt not be overcome".

And all this teaching and this true comfort, it is given

generally, to all my even-christians, as is before said. And such is God's will. This word, "Thou shalt not be overcome", was said full sharply and full mightily, for sureness and comfort against all tribulations that may come. He said not "Thou shalt not be troubled, thou shalt not be travailed, thou shalt not be distressed"; but he said "Thou shalt not be overcome". It is God's will that we take heed to these words, and that we be ever mighty in faithful trust in weal and woe. For he loveth us and liketh us; and so willeth he that we love him and like him, and mightily trust in him. And all shall be well. And then all was finished, and I saw no more.

THE SIXTY-NINTH CHAPTER

Of the Devil's second long temptation to despair

AFTER this, the fiend came again with his heat and his stench, and made me full busy. The stench was so vile and so painful, and the bodily heat so dreadful and hard to bear! Also, I heard talking, bodily, as between two people; and both, to my thinking, talked at once (as though they were in parliament), with great earnestness; and all was soft whispering. And I understood not what they said. All this, it appeared, was to move me to despair; it seemed as though they scornfully imitated the telling of the Beads when they are said with noise of words, with much failing of that devout attention and wise diligence which we owe to God in our prayer. But our good Lord gave me the grace mightily to trust in him, and to comfort my soul with bodily speech—as I might have done for another person who was in distress.

Yet it seemed to me that all this could not be likened to any bodily business.

THE SEVENTIETH CHAPTER

But she trusted mightily in God and in the faith of Holy Church, rehearsing to herself the passion of Christ; by which she was delivered

My bodily eyes I fixed on the same cross (on which I had gazed for my comfort before this time): my tongue I occupied with speech of Christ's passion and with rehearsing the faith of Holy Church: and my heart I fastened on God with all my trust and might. And I thought to myself: "Thou hast now great earnestness about keeping thee in the faith, that thou shouldst not be taken by thine enemies. If now from this time thou shouldst ever more be as busy about keeping thee from sin, this would be a good and sovereign occupation." And I thought: "Truly, were I safe from sin, I would be full safe from all the fiends in hell, and all the enemies of my soul."

And thus the fiends occupied me all that night and in the morning, till it was about nine in the day. And then they were all gone and past, and there was left nothing but a stink, which lasted still a while. I scorned him; and thus was I delivered from him by the power of Christ's passion. For "therewith is the fiend overcome", as our Lord Jesus Christ said before.

In all this blessed shewing, our Lord gave me to understand that sight of it should pass. But the faith keepeth it, with his own good will and his grace. For though he left me with neither sign nor token whereby I might know it; yet he left me with his own blessed word in true understanding, bidding me full mightily that I should believe it. And so I do; blessed may he be! I believe that it is our Saviour that shewed it, and that what he shewed is in the faith. And therefore I love it, ever rejoicing in it; and thereto I am bound—

with all the meaning that he gave, and with the next words that follow: "Keep thee therein and trust thereto". Thus I am bound to keep it in my faith.

Yet on the same day that it was shewed, when the sight of it was passed, as a wretch I forsook it, and openly said that I had raved. But our Lord Jesus, of his mercy, would not let it perish. He shewed it all again within my soul; and with more fullness—with the blessed light of his precious love, saying these words full mightily and full meekly: "Know it now well, that it was no raving that thou saw today". As if he had said: "Because the sight had passed from thee, thou losedst it, and couldst not or mightest not keep it. But know it now." That is to say "now thou seest it". This was said not only for this time, but also that I might set thereupon the ground of my faith—there where he saith in the words immediately following: "but take it and believe it, and keep thee therein and comfort thee therewith, and trust thereto: and thou shalt not be overcome."

THE SEVENTY-FIRST CHAPTER

In all tribulation we must be steadfast in the faith, trusting mightily in God: for if our faith had no enmity it would deserve no meed; and how all these shewings are in the faith

IN these six words that follow where he saith "take it", his meaning is to fasten it faithfully in our heart. For he willeth that it dwell with us, in faith, unto our life's end: and afterwards, in fullness of joy. It is his will that we have ever faithful trust in his blessed promises, knowing his goodness. For our faith is contraried in diverse manners by our own blindness and our ghostly enemy, within and without. And therefore our precious Lover helpeth us with ghostly light and true teaching in diverse manners within and without;

whereby we may know him. And therefore in whatever manner he teacheth us, he willeth that we perceive him wisely, receive him sweetly, and keep us in him faithfully.

Above the faith there is no goodness kept in this life, as to my sight. And beneath the faith there is no health of soul. But in the faith—there willeth our Lord that we keep us. For we are able, by his goodness and his own working, to keep us in the faith. By his sufferance, through ghostly enmity, we are tried in the faith and made mighty. For if our faith had not enmity, it would deserve no meed. Such is the understanding that I have of our Lord's meaning.

Glad and merry and sweet is the blissful lovely looking of our Lord into our souls. For he ever beholdeth us as we live in loving longing; and it is his will that our soul look gladly unto him, to grant him his meed. And thus I hope that he, with his grace, hath brought and shall bring even more, that outward regard into the inward; and make us all at one with him and with each other, in that true lasting Joy which is Jesus.

I have understanding of three lookings of our Lord. The first is the look which he shewed in his passion, whilst he was with us in this life, in his dying. And though this looking is mournful and sorrowful, yet it is glad and merry: because he is God. The second look is of pity and ruth and compassion. And this sheweth he to all his lovers who have need of his mercy, with sureness of keeping. The third is the blissful look, such as shall be without end. And this was oftenest shewed and continued longest.

And thus in the time of our pain and woe, he sheweth us the look that belongeth to his passion and his cross, helping us to bear it by his own blessed power. And in the time of our sinning, he sheweth us the look of ruth and pity, mightily keeping and defending us against all our enemies.

And these two are, commonly, the looks which he sheweth us in this life; with which he mingleth the third (resembling, in part, what it shall be in heaven), by the gracious touching and sweet enlightening of our ghostly life. By that look we are kept in true faith, hope and charity, with contrition and devotion; and also with contemplation and all manner of true joys and sweet comforts. The blissful look of our Lord God worketh all this in us by grace.

THE SEVENTY-SECOND CHAPTER

Sin in chosen souls is deadly for a time: but they are not dead in the sight of God; and we have, here, matter for joy and mourning, because of our blindness and heaviness of the flesh; and of the most comforting look of God; and why these shewings were made

BUT now I needs must tell you in what manner I saw deadly sin in those creatures who would not die because of sin, but would live without end in the joy of God. I saw that two contraries could not be together in one place. The greatest contraries that there are, are the highest bliss and the deepest pain. The highest bliss there is, is to have God in clearness of endless light, him truly seeing, him sweetly feeling, him all perfectly having, in fullness of joy. Thus was this blissful look of our Lord God shewed, in part. In which shewing I saw that sin was its greatest contrary: so far forth that as long as we have anything to do with sin, we shall never see clearly this blissful look of God. And the more horrible and grievous our sins are, the deeper are we, for that time, out of this blessed sight. And therefore it seemeth to us, oftentimes, as though we were in peril of death and in a part of hell; because of the sorrow and pain that sin meaneth to us. And thus we are dead for the time—out of very sight of our blissful life.

But in all this, I saw, in faith, that we are not dead in the sight of God, and he passeth never away from us; though he shall never have his full bliss in us till we have our full bliss in him—truly seeing his fair, blissful look. For we are ordained thereto by kind and brought thereto by grace. Thus I saw how, with regard to those blessed creatures of endless life, sin is deadly for a short time.

Ever the more clearly the soul seeth this blissful look, by grace of loving, the more it longeth to see it in fullness; that is to say, in his own likeness. For notwithstanding that our Lord God dwelleth now in us, and claspeth us and encloseth us, out of tender love, so that he can never leave us and is nearer to us than tongue can tell or heart can think; yet can we never cease from mourning nor from weeping, nor from seeking nor from longing: until we see him clearly with this blissful look of his. (For in that precious sight no woe may abide nor weal fail.)

And in this I saw matter for mirth, and matter for mourning: matter for mirth—that our Lord our Maker is so near to us and in us and we in him, by sureness of keeping, because of his great goodness; matter for mourning—because our ghostly eye is so blind, and we are so borne down by the weight of our mortal flesh and the darkness of sin, that we cannot see our Lord clearly with that blissful look of his. No: and because of this darkness we can scarce believe or trust his great love, and our sureness of keeping. And therefore it is as I say: we can never leave off mourning or weeping. Weeping here meaneth not merely the pouring out of tears from our bodily eye; but also unto a more ghostly understanding. For the kindly desire of our soul is so great and so unmeasurable, that if all the nobility that God ever made in heaven and in earth were given to us for our joy and comfort, apart from the sight of this fair blissful look of his; yet we would never take leave of mourning or ghostly weeping (that is to say painful longing), until we saw verily this fair blissful look of our Maker. And if we were to suffer all the pain that heart can think or tongue can tell, and we could, in that time, see this blissful look: all that pain would not grieve us.

Thus is that blissful sight the end of all manner of pain unto loving souls, and full filling of all manner of joy and bliss. And that shewed he in the high marvellous words where he saith: "I it am that is highest: I it am that thou lovest: I it am that is all". It belongeth to us to have three knowings. The first is that we know our Lord God. The second is that we know ourselves—what we are by him, in kind and in grace. The third is that we know meekly what we are with regard to our sin and our feebleness. And for these three was made all this shewing, as I understand it.

THE SEVENTY-THIRD CHAPTER

These Revelations were shown triple-wise; and of a double ghostly sureness: through which it is God's will that we amend us, remembering his passion, knowing also that he is all love, without unreasonable heaviness for our past sins

ALL this blessed teaching of our Lord God was shewed in three ways: that is to say, by bodily sight, and by words formed in my understanding, and by ghostly sight. Of the bodily sight I have told as I saw, as truly as I can. And as regards the words, I have told them just as our Lord shewed them to me. Of the ghostly sight, I have spoken somewhat, but I can never explain it fully. Therefore of this ghostly sight I am moved to say more, as far as God will give me grace.

God shewed two sorts of sickness that we have: the one is impatience or sloth, in that we bear our travail and our pain heavily: the other is despair or doubtful dread, as I shall say afterwards. Sin he shewed in general (in which all special sins are comprehended); but he shewed none but these two in particular. It is these two that most exercise and trouble us, as our Lord shewed me; of which it is his will that we be amended (I mean those men and women who, for God's love, hate sin, and dispose themselves to do God's will.)

By our ghostly blindness, then, and our bodily heaviness we are most inclined to these two. And therefore it is God's will that they be known; and then we should reject them, as we do other sins. And as help against them, our Lord shewed full meekly the patience that he had in his hard passion; and also the joy and the liking that he hath of that passion, for love. And this he shewed as an example, that we should gladly and lightly bear our pains; for that is most pleasing to him, and of endless profit to us. And the reason why we are exercised over these things is because of unknowing of love. (For though the three Persons of the blessed Trinity are co-equal, yet the soul had most understanding of Love.) Yea, and it is his will that we have our beholding and our enjoyment in Love. And yet concerning this knowing we are most blind. For some of us believe that God is almighty and may do all; and that he is all-wisdom and can do all; but that he is all-love, and will do all—there we fail.

It is this unknowing that most hindereth God's lovers, as I see it. For even when we begin to hate sin, and to amend us by ordinance of Holy Church, there dwelleth in us a dread that is an hindrance to us, through the beholding of our selves and our sins committed in the past. Because of our sins of every day, because we (or some of us) hold not to our promise, nor keep to the cleanness that our Lord setteth us in, but fall oftentimes into so much wretchedness that it is shame to us to mention it—the beholding of this maketh us so sorrowful and so heavy that we can scarcely see any comfort.

This dread we mistake sometimes for meekness. But it is a foul blindness and a wickedness. And yet we cannot despise it as we do any other sin that we recognize, though it cometh through lack of judgement, and is against truth. It is God's will that, of all the properties of the blessed Trinity, we have the greatest sureness and liking in love. For love maketh might and wisdom full meek to us. For just as, by his courtesy, God forgetteth our sin after the time that we repent us, so it is his will that we forget our sin, in respect of our stupid heaviness, and our doubtful dread.

THE SEVENTY-FOURTH CHAPTER

There are four sorts of dread; but reverent dread is a lovely, true dread that is never without meek love: yet these two are not the same; and how we should pray for them

FOR I have understanding of four sorts of dread. One is that state of fear which cometh upon a man suddenly in his frailty. This dread doeth good, because it helpeth to purge a man, as doth sickness or any other pain that is not sin. All such pains help a man if they are patiently accepted. The second is the dread of pain, by which a man is stirred up and awakened from the sleep of sin. For the man that is hard asleep in sin is not able, at the time, to receive the soft strengthening of the Holy Ghost until he hath felt this fear of pain, of bodily death, and of ghostly enemies. This dread moveth us to seek comfort and mercy of God. And thus this dread helpeth us as giving us an entry, enabling us to come to contrition through the blissful touching of the Holy Ghost.

The third is doubtful dread. In as much as it leadeth to despair, God willeth to have it turned into love in us, by true knowing of love; that is to say, that the bitterness of doubt be turned into the sweetness of kind love, by grace. For it can never please our Lord that his servants doubt in his goodness.

The fourth is reverent dread. There is no dread in us that fully pleaseth God, but reverent dread. It is full soft; for the more it is had, the less it is felt, because of the sweetness of love. Love and dread are brethren; and they are rooted in us by the goodness of our Maker; they shall never be taken from us without end. It belongeth to us, of kind, to love; and of grace, to love; and of kind, to dread; and of grace, to dread. It belongeth to the Lordship and to the Fatherhood to be dreaded, as it belongeth to the Goodness to be loved. And it belongeth to us that are his servants and his children to dread him in his Lordship and Fatherhood, as it belongeth to us to love him in Goodness. And though this reverent dread and love are not both-in-one, but two in property and in working, yet neither of them may be had without the other. And therefore I am sure that he who loveth, dreadeth—though he feels it but little.

All dreads, other than reverent dread, which are proffered to us are not truly holy, though they come to us under colour of holiness. And hereby they can be known separately. The dread that maketh us hastily to fly from all that is not good unto our Lord's breast, like the child into its mother's lap, with all our will and with all our mind; knowing our feebleness and our great need, knowing his everlasting goodness and his great love; seeking unto him only for salvation, cleaving to him with sure trust—the dread that bringeth us into this working, it is kind and gracious, good and true. And all that is contrary to it, it is either wrong, or is mingled with wrong. Then is this the remedy—to recognize them both, and reject the wrong.

For the kind property of dread, which we have in this life by the gracious working of the Holy Ghost, the same shall be, in heaven, before God, gentle, courteous and full sweet. And thus we shall, in love, be homely and near to God, and in dread, gentle and courteous to God: both qualities united equally. Desire we then, of our Lord God, to dread him reverently and love him meekly and trust in him mightily. For when we dread him reverently and love him meekly, our trust is never in vain. For the more that we trust and the more mightily that we trust, the more we please and worship our Lord in whom we trust. And if we fail in this reverent dread and meek love (God forbid that we should!), our trust is at once misruled for that time. And therefore we greatly need to pray our Lord for grace, that we may have this reverent dread and meek love, of his gift, in heart and in work. For without this no man can please God.

THE SEVENTY-FIFTH CHAPTER

We need love, longing and pity; and of three sorts of longing in God, which are in us; and how, in the Day of Doom, the joy of the blessed shall be increased: seeing truly the cause of all that God hath done, trembling with awe and giving thanks with joy, marvelling at the greatness of God, and the littleness of all that is made

I SAW that God can do all that we need. These three we need: love, longing and pity. Pity and love keep us in the time of our need. And the longing in the same love draweth us unto heaven. For God thirsteth to have all-man, generally, in himself. In which thirst he hath drawn up all his holy souls that are now in bliss. And in gaining his living members, ever he draweth up and drinketh; and yet he still thirsteth and longeth.

I saw three sorts of longing in God, all directed to one end. The first is that he longeth to teach us to know him and to love him ever more and more, as is proper and expedient to us. The second is that he longeth to have us up into bliss, as souls are when they are taken out of pain into heaven. The third is, to fill us full of bliss; and that shall be fulfilled on the last day, to last for ever. For I saw (even as it is known in our faith) that then, pain and sorrow shall be ended in all that shall be saved. And we shall receive not merely the same bliss that souls in heaven had before, but we shall also receive a new bliss, which shall flow plenteously out of God into us, and fill us full. These are the goods which he hath ordained to give us from without-beginning. These goods are treasured and hid in himself. And unto that time the creature is not powerful or worthy enough to receive them.

In this we shall see truly the cause of all the deeds that God hath done. And ever more we shall see the cause of all the things that he hath permitted. The bliss and the fulfilment shall be so deep and high that, for wonder and marvel, all creatures shall have towards God a reverent dread so greatly overpassing that which was seen and felt before, that the pillars of heaven shall tremble and quake. But this manner of trembling and dread shall contain no manner of pain; for it belongeth to the worthy majesty of God thus to be beheld by his creatures, with aweful trembling and quaking—but much more for joy, endlessly marvelling at the greatness of the Maker, and at the least part of all that is made. For the beholding of this maketh the creature marvellously meek and mild.

Wherefore it is God's will, and also it belongeth to us

both in kind and in grace, to understand and to know this, desiring this sight and this working. For it leadeth us in the right way, and keepeth us in true life, and oneth us to God. And as good as God is, even so great is he. And as much as it belongeth to his Godhead to be loved, so much it belongeth to his great highness to be dreaded. For this reverent dread is the fairest courtesy that is in heaven, before God's face. And as much as he shall be known and loved, overpassing what he is now; in so much he shall be dreaded, overpassing what he is now. Wherefore it needs must be that all heaven and all earth shall tremble and quake, when the pillars shall tremble and quake.

THE SEVENTY-SIXTH CHAPTER

A loving soul hateth sin, for its vileness, more than all the pain of hell; and how the beholding of other men's sins (except it be with compassion) hindereth the beholding of God; and the Devil, by putting into our remembrance our wretchedness, would be hindrance to the same; and of our sloth

I SPEAK but little of this reverent dread, for I hope it may be seen in the matter told before; but I am certain that our Lord shewed me no souls except those that dread him. And well I know that the soul that truly taketh the teaching of the Holy Ghost hateth sin for its vileness and horribleness more than it doth all the pain that is in hell. For the soul that beholdeth the goodness of our Lord Jesus hateth no hell but sin, as I see it. And therefore it is God's will that we should know sin, and pray earnestly and labour willingly, and seek teaching meekly so that we fall not blindly therein.

The soul that will be at rest, when other men's sins come to mind, should flee from them as from the pains of hell. For the beholding of other men's sins maketh, as it were, a thick mist before the eye of the soul; so that we cannot, for the time, see the fairness of God—unless we behold them with contrition along with the sinner, with compassion on him and with holy desire to God for him. For without this they annoy and trouble and hinder the soul that beholdeth them. This is my understanding of the shewing of the compassion.

In this blissful shewing of our Lord, I have understanding of two contraries: one is, the highest wisdom that a man may achieve in this life, the other is, the most folly. The highest wisdom is for a creature to do according to the will and counsel of his highest sovereign Friend. This blessed Friend is Jesus; and it is his will and counsel that we hold us with him, and fasten us, homely, to him evermore—in what state so ever we be. For whether we be foul or clean, we are ever one in his loving. Neither for weal nor for woe is it his will that we ever flee from him; but because of our changeability we fall often into sin. Then are we affected by the promptings of our enemy, and by our own folly and blindness. For they say thus: "Thou knowest well thou art a wretch and a sinner, and also untrue, for thou keepest not thy covenant. Thou hast promised oftentimes our Lord that thou shalt do better. And immediately thou fallest again into the same sins—especially into sloth and the wasting of time." (For this is the beginning of sin, as I see it, particularly in creatures that have given themselves to serve our Lord by inward beholding of his blissful goodness.) And this maketh us adread to appear before our courteous Lord. Then it is that our enemy will abash us with this false dread of our wretchedness and the pain that he threateneth us with. For it is his intent to make us so heavy and so mournful in this that we let pass out of mind the blissful beholding of our everlasting Friend.

THE SEVENTY-SEVENTH CHAPTER

Of the enmity of the fiend, who loseth more in our uprising than he winneth by our falling: and therefore is he scorned; and how the scourge of God should be suffered with mind of his passion: for that is specially rewarded, above the penance chosen by ourselves; and we must needs have woe; but courteous God is our Leader, Keeper and Bliss

Our good Lord shewed the enmity of the fiend; whereby I understood that all that is contrary to love and peace is of the fiend and his company. And it belongeth to our feebleness and our folly to fall; and it belongeth to the mercy and grace that we have of the Holy Ghost to rise to more joy. And if our enemy winneth aught from us by our falling (and this is his pleasure), he loseth many times more in our rising through charity and meekness. This glorious rising is to him such great sorrow and pain (for the hatred that he hath to our souls) that he burneth continually in envy. And all this sorrow that he would make us have shall turn against himself. And for this reason it was that our Lord scorned him, and shewed that he shall be scorned; and this made me mightily to laugh.

This then is the remedy—that we be aware of our wretchedness, and flee to our Lord. For ever the more needy that we be, the more speedful it is for us to touch him. And let us say thus, in our meaning: "I know well that I have deserved pain. But our Lord is almighty, and may punish me mightily, and he is all-wisdom, and can punish me wisely; and he is all-goodness, and loveth me tenderly." And in this beholding it is speedful to us to abide. For it is a full lovely meekness in a sinful soul, wrought by the mercy and grace of the Holy Ghost, when we are willing, willfully and gladly, to take the scourging and chastising that our Lord himself will give us. And this shall be full tender and full easy, if only we hold us pleased with him and with all his works. But concerning the penance that a man should take upon himself—this was not shewed me: that is to say, it was not shewed me specifically. But this other was shewed, specially and highly and with a look full of love—that we should meekly and patiently bear and suffer the penance that God giveth us, with mind of his blessed passion. For when we have mind of his blessed passion, with pity and love, then we suffer with him like as did his friends that saw it.

And this was shewed in the thirteenth Revelation, near the beginning where it speaketh of pity. For he saith: "Accuse not thyself that thy tribulation and thy woe is all thy fault. For it is not my will that thou shouldst be heavy and sorrowful without discretion. For I tell thee: howsoever thou doest, thou shalt have woe. And therefore it is my will that thou wisely know the penance which thou art in continually—that thou mayest meekly take it for thy penance. And then shalt thou truly see that all this thy living is profitable penance." This place is a prison: this life is a penance. And in the remedy for it, he willeth that we rejoice. The remedy is that our Lord is with us, keeping us, and leading us to fullness of joy.

For this is endless joy to us, in our Lord's meaning, that he that shall be our bliss when we come there—he is our keeper while we are here, our way and our heaven in true love and faithful trust. And of this he gave understanding in all, and especially in the shewing of his passion, where he made me mightily to choose him for my heaven. Flee we to our Lord, and we shall be comforted. Touch we him, and we shall be made clean. Cling we to him, and we shall be secure and safe from all manner of perils. For our courteous Lord willeth that we be as homely with him as heart can think or soul can desire.

But we must beware lest we take this homeliness so recklessly as to forsake courtesy. Our Lord himself is sovereign Homeliness. But as homely as he is, even so courteous he is; for he is very Courtesy. And the blessed creatures that shall be in heaven with him without end—these he will have like unto himself in all things. To be like our Lord perfectly, this is our very salvation and our full bliss. And if we know not how we shall bear ourselves, let us desire this of our Lord, and he shall teach us; for this is to his own liking and his worship. Blessed may he be!

THE SEVENTY-EIGHTH CHAPTER

Our Lord willeth that we know of four manners of goodness that he doeth to us; and how we need the light of grace to know our sin and feebleness: for we are nothing of ourselves but wretchedness; and we cannot know the horror of sin as it is; and how our enemy would that we should never know our sin until the last day: wherefore we are meekly indebted to God that sheweth it now

OUR Lord of his mercy sheweth us our sin and our feebleness, by the sweet gracious light of himself. For our sin is so foul and horrible that he, of his courtesy, willeth not to shew it us except by the light of his mercy. It is his will that we have knowing of four things: the first is, that he is the ground, of whom we have all our life and our being; the second is, that he keepeth us mightily and mercifully during the time that we are in our sin, amongst all the enemies that come full fiercely upon us (we are so much the more in peril because we give them occasion, and know not our own need); the third is, how courteously he keepeth us, and maketh us to know that we go amiss; the fourth is how steadfastly he abideth us, and changeth not his regard. For it is his will that we be converted and oned to him in love, as he is to us. And thus, by his gracious knowing, we can see that our sin is profitable, without despairing. For truly we need to see it; and by the sight we should be made ashamed of ourselves, and broken down with regard to our pride and presumption. For it behoveth us truly to see that of ourselves we are right naught but sin and wretchedness.

And thus, by the sight of the less which our Lord sheweth us, the greater, which we see not, is laid waste. For he, of his courtesy, tempereth the sight to us. For it is so foul and horrible that we could not endure to see it as it is. And thus, by this meek knowing, through sorrow and contrition, we shall be broken off from all things that are not our Lord. And then shall our blessed Saviour perfectly heal us and one us to himself.

This breaking and this healing our Lord meaneth for men in general. For he that is highest and nearest to God, can see himself as sinful and needy as I do. And I, that am the least and lowest of those that shall be saved, can be comforted along with him that is highest. Even so hath our Lord oned us in charity. When he shewed me that I should sin, for the joy that I had in beholding him, I did not attend readily to that shewing. But our courteous Lord let it rest there, and desired to teach me no further, until he gave me the grace and will to attend. And here I was taught that though we be lifted high into contemplation by the special gift of our Lord, yet it behoveth us therewith to have knowing and sight of our sin and of our feebleness. For without this knowing we cannot be safe. And also I saw that we cannot have this knowing of ourselves, or of our ghostly enemies (for they do not wish us so much good; and if it depended on their will, we should never see it till our dying day). Thus we are much indebted to God that he desireth himself, for love, to shew it us in the time of mercy and of grace.

THE SEVENTY-NINTH CHAPTER

We are taught concerning our own sin, and not our neighbours'—except for their help; and God willeth we know that whatsoever prompting we have contrary to this shewing cometh from our enemy; because we know the great love of God we must not be more careless about falling; and if we fall, we must hastily rise—else we are greatly unkind to God

ALSO in this I had more understanding of that shewing where he shewed me that I should sin. I had taken it simply as referring to my own single person; for I was not otherwise prompted in that time. But by the high gracious comfort of our Lord that followed after, I saw that his meaning was for man in general: that is to say all-man, which is sinful and shall be unto the last day. Of which man I am a member (as I hope) by the mercy of God. For the blessed comfort that I saw is large enough for all. And there was I learned that I should look at my own sin and not other men's, except it be for comfort or help of my even-christians. And also, in the same shewing where I saw that I should sin, there was I learned to be full of dread for unsureness of myself. For I know not how I shall fall; and I know not the measure nor the greatness of my sin. For that would I have found out, full of dread; and thereto I had no answer.

Also our courteous Lord, in that same time, shewed full sweetly and full mightily the endlessness and immutability of his love; and also his great goodness and his gracious inward keeping—that the love of him and of our souls shall never be separated unto without-end. And thus in the dread

I have occasion for meekness, which saveth me from presumption; and in the blessed shewing of love I have matter of true comfort and of joy, which saveth me from despair.

All this homely shewing of our courteous Lord is a lovely lesson and a sweet gracious teaching from himself, in the comforting of our soul. For it is his will that we know, by the sweetness of the homely love of him, that all that we see or feel, within or without, which is contrary to this, that it is of the enemy and not of God. So that if we be prompted to be the more careless in our living or in the keeping of our heart because we have knowing of this plenteous love: then we need greatly to beware of this prompting. If it come, it is untrue, and greatly ought we to hate it; for it hath no resemblance to God's will.

And when we are fallen by frailty or blindness, then our courteous Lord toucheth us, prompteth us and keepeth us. And then willeth he that we see our wretchedness, and meekly acknowledge it. But it is not his will that we busy ourselves greatly about our accusing, nor that we be too full of wretchedness about ourselves. Rather he willeth that we hastily turn unto him; for he standeth all alone and abideth us continually in our mourning and moaning, until we come. He hath haste to have us turn to him; for we are his joy and his delight, and he is the health of our life. (Where I say "He standeth all alone", I speak not of the blessed company in heaven, but I speak of his office and working here in earth—according to the manner of the shewing.)

THE EIGHTIETH CHAPTER

By three things God is worshipped and we saved; and how our knowing is but an ABC: and sweet Jesus doeth all, abiding and mourning with us; but when we are in sin Christ mourneth alone: then it belongeth to us, for kindness and reverence, hastily to turn again to him

By three things man standeth in this life; by which three God is worshipped, and we are sped, kept and saved. The first is use of man's kindly reason; the second is the common teaching of Holy Church; the third is the inward gracious working of the Holy Ghost—and these three are all of one God. God is the ground of our kindly reason; and God is the teaching of Holy Church; and God is the Holy Ghost. And all are sundry gifts, to which he willeth that we have great regard, attending thereto. For they work in us continually, all together; they are great things. Of which greatness he willeth that we have knowing here—the ABC of them, as it were. That is to say, that we may have a little knowing of that whose fullness we shall have in heaven: which is for our profit.

We know in our faith that God alone took our kind, and none but he; and furthermore that Christ alone did all the great works that belong to our salvation, and none but he. And even so he alone doeth now, in the last end; that is to say, he dwelleth here in us, and ruleth us and guideth us in this life, and bringeth us to his bliss. And thus shall he do, as long as any soul is in earth, that shall come to heaven; and so far forth, that if there were no such soul in earth but one, he would be with that one, all alone, until he had brought it up to his bliss.

I believe and understand the ministrations of Holy Angels, as theologians tell; but this was not shewed to me. For himself is nearest and meekest, highest and lowest, and doeth all —and not only all—that we need: but also he doeth all that is worshipful to our joy in heaven. And where I say he abideth us in our mourning and moaning, this meaneth all the true feeling that we have in ourselves of contrition and of compassion, and all the mourning and moaning that we are not oned with our Lord. And in as much as it is profitable it is Christ in us. And though some of us feel it seldom, it passeth never from Christ, till what time he hath brought us out of all our woe. For love suffereth him never to be without pity. And what time that we fall into sin, and leave mind of him and keeping of our own soul; then beareth Christ, alone, all the charge of us. And thus standeth he, mourning and moaning. Then it belongeth to us, for reverence and kindness, to turn us quickly to our Lord, and leave him not alone. He is here alone with us all. That is to say: he is here only for us. And what time I am a stranger to him by sin, despair or sloth, then I let my Lord stand alone, in as much as he is in me. And thus it fareth with all of us who are sinners. And though it be so—that oftentimes we do thus—yet his goodness suffereth us never to be alone; but lastingly he is with us, and tenderly he excuseth, and ever shieldeth us from blame in his sight.

THE EIGHTY-FIRST CHAPTER

This blessed woman saw God in diverse manners: but she saw him take no resting-place but in man's soul; and he willeth that we have more enjoying in his love, than sorrowing for often falling; remembering reward everlasting, and living gladly in penance; and why God permitteth sin

OUR good Lord shewed himself to his creature in diverse

manners, both in heaven and in earth. But I saw him take no place but in man's soul. He shewed himself in earth in the sweet incarnation and his blessed passion; and in another manner he shewed himself in earth—where I saw God in a point; and in another manner he shewed himself in earth— thus as it were in pilgrimage. (That is to say, he is here with us, leading us: and shall be, until he hath brought us all to his bliss, in heaven.) He shewed himself diverse times reigning, as it is aforesaid: but principally in man's soul. He hath taken there his resting-place and his worshipful city. Out of which worshipful see he shall never rise nor remove, without-end.

Marvellous and stately is the place where the Lord dwelleth. And therefore he willeth that we readily turn us to his gracious touching, having more joy in his all-love than sorrow in our frequent fallings. For of anything that we may do, it is most worship to him that we live, in our penance, gladly and merrily for his love. For he beholdeth us so tenderly that he seeth all our living here to be a penance. For the kind longing in us for him is a lasting penance in us. Which penance he worketh in us, and mercifully helpeth us to bear it. For his love maketh him to long; his wisdom and his truth, with his righteousness, maketh him to suffer us here; and in this manner he willeth to see it in us. For this is our kindly penance, as to my sight. This penance never goeth from us till what time that we be full filled, and have him for our meed. And therefore he willeth that we set our hearts in our out-passing: that is to say, from the pain that we feel into the bliss that we trust to have.

THE EIGHTY-SECOND CHAPTER

God beholdeth the moaning of the soul with pity and not with blame: and yet we do naught but sin, in the which we are kept in solace and in dread; for he willeth that we turn us to him, readily cleaving to his love, and seeing that he is our medicine; and so we must love, in longing and in enjoying; and whatsoever is contrary to this is not of God but of enmity

But here shewed our courteous Lord the mourning and the moaning of our soul, meaning thus: "I know well thou willest to live for my love alone, gladly suffering all the penance that may come to thee. But inasmuch as thou livest not without sin, therefore thou art heavy and sorrowful. And if thou couldst live without sin, thou wouldst suffer, for my love, all the woe that might come to thee. And this is sooth. But be not too much grieved with the sin that falleth to thee against thy will."

And here I understand how the Lord beheld the servant with pity and not with blame. For this passing life asketh not to live all without sin. He loveth us endlessly; and we sin habitually; and he sheweth it us full mildly; and then we sorrow and mourn with discretion, turning us into the beholding of his mercy, cleaving to his love and to his goodness; seeing that he is our medicine, realizing that we do naught but sin. And thus by the meekness that we get, in this sight of our sin, faithfully knowing his everlasting love, him thanking and him praising, we please him. "I love thee and thou lovest me, and our love shall never be parted in two."

And all this was shewed in ghostly understanding, seeing this blessed word "I keep thee full surely". And by the great desire that I saw in our blessed Lord, that we should live in this manner—that it to say, in longing and in enjoying, as all this lesson of love sheweth, thereby I understood that all that is contrary to this is not of him, but it is of enmity. And it is his will that we know it, by the sweet gracious light of his kind love.

If there is any living on earth such as is continually kept from falling, I know not of it; for it was not shewed me. But this was shewed: that in falling and in rising we are preciously kept in the same love. For in the beholding of God we fall not, and in the beholding of ourselves we stand not. And both these be truth, as I see it. But the beholding of our Lord God is the higher truth. Then are we much indebted to him, that he willeth, in this life, to shew us this high truth. It is full profitable to us that we see these both at once. For the higher beholding keepeth us in ghostly joy, and true enjoying in God. The other, that is, the lower beholding, keepeth us in dread, and maketh us ashamed of ourselves. But our good Lord willeth ever that we hold us much more in the beholding of the higher, and yet not leave the knowing of the lower, until the time that we be brought up above, where we shall have our Lord Jesus to our meed, and be filled full of joy and bliss without end.

THE EIGHTY-THIRD CHAPTER

Of three properties in God, life, love and light; and that our reason is in God, in accord: it is the highest gift; and how our faith is a light, coming of the Father, measured to us, and in this night us leading; and in the end of our woe, suddenly our eye shall be opened in full light and clarity of sight; which is our Maker, Father and Holy Ghost, in Jesus our Saviour

I HAD, in a measure, touching, sight and feeling in three properties of God. In which the strength and the effect of all Revelation standeth. And they were seen in every shewing;

and most directly in the twelfth, where it is said often: "I it am." The properties are these: life, love and light. In life is marvellous homeliness: in love is gentle courtesy: and in light is endless kindhood. These three properties were seen in one goodness; into which goodness my reason would be oned—cleaving to it with all its might. I beheld with reverent dread, highly marvelling in the sight and in the feeling of the sweet accord—that our reason is in God, understanding that it is the highest gift that we have received: and it is grounded in Kind.

Our faith is a light, kindly coming from our endless Day that is our Father God. In which light our Mother Christ and our good Lord the Holy Ghost lead us, in this passing life. This light is measured discerningly, standing unto us, at need, in the night. The light is the cause of our life: the night is the cause of our pain and all our woe. For which woe we deserve endless meed and thanks from God. For we, with mercy and grace, willfully know and believe our light, going therein wisely and mightily. And at the end of woe, suddenly our eye shall be opened, and in clearness of sight our light shall be full. Which light is God, our Maker, Father, and Holy Ghost in Christ Jesus our Saviour. Thus I saw and understood that our faith is our light in our night. Which light is God, our endless Day.

THE EIGHTY-FOURTH CHAPTER

Charity is this light; which is not so little as not to merit, with labour, endless worshipful thanks of God; for faith and hope lead us to charity, which is in three manners

THIS light is charity; and the measuring of this light is done to us profitably by the wisdom of God. For neither is the light so large that we can see clearly our blissful day, nor is it all shut out from us. But it is a light such as we may live in profitably with labour—deserving the worshipful thanks of God. And this was seen in the sixth shewing, where he saith: "I thank thee for thy service and for thy labour."

Thus charity keepeth us in faith and in hope. And faith and hope lead us into charity. And at the end, all shall be charity. I had three manners of understandings in this light of charity. The first is charity unmade: the second is charity made: the third is charity given. Charity unmade is God: charity made is our soul in God: charity given is the virtue. And that is a gracious gift, in the working of which we love God for himself and ourselves in God and all that God loveth, for God.

THE EIGHTY-FIFTH CHAPTER

God loved his chosen from without-beginning, and he never suffereth them to be hurt in a way that their bliss might be lessened; and how secrets now hid in heaven shall be known: whereof we shall bless our Lord that everything is so well ordained

AND in this sight I marvelled highly. For notwithstanding our simpleness and our blindness here, our Lord endlessly beholdeth us, rejoicing in this working. And we can please him best of all by believing this truly, and rejoicing with him and in him. For as truly as we shall be in the bliss of God without end, him praising and thanking; so truly we have been in the foreknowledge of God, loved and known in his endless purpose from without-beginning. In which unbegun love he made us, and in the same love he keepeth us, and never suffereth us to be hurt in a way that our bliss might be lessened. And therefore, when judgement is given, and we are all brought up above, then shall we clearly see in God the secrets which now are hid from us. And then none of us shall be prompted to say of anything: "Lord, if it had been thus, it had been well"; but we shall all say with one voice: "Lord, blessed may thou be! For it is thus, and it is well. Now we see truly that all thing is done as was thine ordinance before anything was made."

THE EIGHTY-SIXTH CHAPTER

The good Lord shewed that this book should be completed otherwise than at its first writing. And he willeth that for his working we should pray thus: him thanking, trusting, and in him enjoying; and how he made this shewing because he willeth to have it known: in which knowing he will give us grace to love him: for fifteen years afterwards, it was answered that the cause of this shewing was love: which love may Jesus grant us.
Amen

THIS book is begun by God's gift and his grace; but it is not yet performed, as I see it. For charity's sake, let us pray all together with God's working, thanking, trusting, enjoying. For it is thus that our good Lord willeth us to pray, according to the understanding that I took in all his meaning, and in the sweet words that he said full merrily "I am ground of thy beseeching". For I saw truly and understood in our Lord's meaning that he shewed it because he will have it known more than it is. In which knowing he will give us grace to love him and cleave to him. For he beheld his heavenly treasure with so great love on earth, that he willeth to give more light and solace in heavenly joy, in drawing our hearts from the sorrow and darkness which we are in.

And from the time that it was shewed, I desired oftentimes to know what was our Lord's meaning in it. And fifteen years after, and more, I was answered in ghostly understanding: "What, wouldst thou know thy Lord's meaning in this thing? Know it well. Love was his meaning. Who sheweth it thee? Love. Wherefore sheweth he it thee? For Love. Hold thee therein. Thou shalt know more in the same, but thou shalt never know other therein, without end."

Thus was I learned that love is our Lord's meaning. And I saw full surely in this, and in all, that before God made us, he loved us. Which love was never slaked, nor ever shall be. And in this love he hath done all his works. And in this love he hath made all things profitable to us. And in this love our life is everlasting. In our making we had beginning: but the love wherein he made us was in him from without-beginning. In which love we have our beginning. And all this shall we see in God without end.

Thanks be to God.

Here endeth the Book of Revelations of Julian, the Anchoress of Norwich. On whose soul may God have mercy.

COLOPHON

I pray almighty God that this book come only to the hands of them that will be his faithful lovers, and to them that will submit them to the faith of Holy Church, and obey the wholesome understanding and teaching of men that be of virtuous life, sober years and profound learning. For this Revelation is high divinity, and high wisdom; wherefore it cannot dwell with him who is a thrall to sin and to the Devil. And beware that thou take not one thing and leave another, according to thy affection and liking—for that is the way of an heretic; but take everything with other, truly understanding that all is according to Holy Scripture, and grounded in the same. This Jesus, our very love, light and truth, shall shew to all clean souls that, with meekness, ask perseveringly of him this wisdom. And thou to whom this book shall come, thank highly and heartily our Saviour Christ Jesus, that he made these shewings and revelations for thee and to thee, of his endless love, mercy and goodness, for thine and our safe guide and conduct to everlasting bliss. The which may Jesus grant us. Amen.

Here end the sublime and wonderful Revelations of the unutterable love of God in Jesus Christ, vouchsafed to a dear lover of his, and, in her, to all his dear friends and lovers; whose hearts, like hers, burn in the love of our dearest Jesus.